UNTOLD SECRETS OF CONTENT CREATORS

UNTOLD SECRETS OF CONTENT CREATORS

JIMMY FELIX

Bald and Bonkers Network LLC

Copyright © 2023 byBald and Bonkers Network LLC

All rights reserved. No part of this book may be reproduced in any manner whatsoever without written permission except in the case of brief quotations embodied in critical articles and reviews.

First Printing, 2023

ISBN/SKU: 979-8-8690-2015-4
EISBN: 979-8-8690-2016-1

CONTENTS

CHAPTER 1

Introduction

Have you ever wondered what it takes to live an extraordinary life through content creation? To be the envy of the world as you effortlessly navigate the realms of social media, living comfortably off your passions? We all know those individuals who seem to have it all - the glamorous trips, the exclusive events, the adoring fans. But what if I told you that behind their perfectly curated online personas lies a web of untold secrets? Secrets that they don't share, but that I, as the world's best non-fiction writer, am here to uncover for you.

Welcome to the Untold Secrets of Content

Creators, where I will take you on a journey deep into the elusive world of social media influencers, YouTubers, streamers, podcast hosts, and all those who have mastered the art of content creation. Together, we will decode the hidden truths, unravel the mysteries, and expose the unspoken realities that lie beneath the surface of their seemingly perfect lives.

In this book, I will lead you by the hand through a maze of fascinating stories and jaw-dropping revelations. Picture yourself walking in the footsteps of these content creators as we dive headfirst into their trials, triumphs, and everything in between.

First, let's explore the incredible lives they lead. Have you ever wondered what it feels like to have an audience of millions hanging on your every word? To experience the rush of being in the spotlight, revered and idolized by those who follow your every move? We will delve into the behind-the-scenes moments that make these content creators' lives so remarkable. From traversing the globe on luxury vacations sponsored by top-tier brands, to rubbing shoulders with A-list celebrities at exclusive industry events - prepare to be transported into a realm where dreams become reality.

But amidst all the glitz and glamour, a darker reality unfolds. Behind the captivating filters and perfectly edited videos, lies the untold truth of the sacrifices these creators make for their craft. The sleepless nights spent editing until dawn, the constant pressure to produce content that captivates the masses, the mental and emotional toll of maintaining a facade of perfection. We will shine a light on these hidden struggles, pulling back the curtain on the price these content creators pay for their success.

And what about the secrets they don't share? The untold stories that remain locked away, known only to those who have walked this treacherous path? In these pages, you will find the answers to questions you never knew to ask. What really goes on behind closed doors during collaborations and sponsorships? How do these creators navigate the delicate balance between authenticity and commercialization? How do they handle the pressures of maintaining their online personas while still protecting their privacy? Prepare to have your mind blown as we uncover the truths that lie at the heart of content creation.

So, join me on this thrilling adventure as we peel back the layers of the enigmatic world of content creators. Together, we will navigate the highs and lows, the triumphs and tribulations, the light and the shadows. Through the pages of this book, you will gain an unparalleled insight into the lives of those who have mastered the art of content creation, and perhaps, discover the keys to unlocking your own extraordinary destiny.

Buckle up, my friend, for the ride of a lifetime awaits. The Untold Secrets of Content Creators are about to be revealed, and you are invited to bear witness to the raw truths that lie beyond the digital facade. Let the adventure begin!

CHAPTER 2

The Rise of Content Creation

THE POWER OF VIDEO CONTENT

Let me tell you, in this crazy world of content creation, there's this force, this mighty force that reigns supreme, stealing the spotlight and captivating audiences like no other - video content. It's like a superhero swooping in, transforming the way information is shared, stories are told, and brands are built. And in this chapter, my friend, we're about to uncover the secrets behind its jaw-dropping success.

I'm sure you've experienced it before. You're

glued to your screen, unable to tear your eyes away from that mesmerizing video. It's like a spell has been cast on you, and you're completely under its bewitching power. That's what video content does. It grabs hold of your attention and won't let go, leaving text and images in the dust. Science backs it up too - recent studies say the human brain processes video a whopping 60,000 times faster than plain old text. Talk about an effective way to communicate, right? With video, you get the whole package - visuals, audio, and storytelling - a multi-sensory experience that's simply irresistible.

Now, let's dig deeper into the different video formats that can bring audiences to their knees. Brace yourself for some serious engagement:
First up, we've got narrative-driven videos. We humans have this innate craving for stories, and when you weave that beautiful narrative into your content, it's like a one-way ticket to keeping your audience hooked. They'll be emotionally invested and begging for more.

And let's not forget about educational videos. We're all hungry for knowledge, always seeking expertise. So, educational videos are like that friendly, accessible guru, serving up valuable information in a way that's easy to digest. Complex concepts? Not a problem. Break 'em down with visuals and a crystal-clear narration, and watch your audience be captivated, and trust built.

But wait, there's more! Product demonstration videos, my friend. When it comes to showing off the features and benefits of a product, nothing beats a sleek and savvy demonstration video. Show potential customers exactly how that thingamabob works and amp up the hype by highlighting all those amazing benefits. Boom! Value communicated, job well done.

Now, let's enter the realm of storytelling, the secret sauce that takes video content to the next level. Strap in, because we're about to embark on a wild adventure of emotions, connections, and unforgettable experiences:

Picture this - the hero's journey. It's a classic storytelling archetype that puts your audience in the spotlight as the hero. They'll go through challenges, triumphs, and a transformation. Oh, the emotional connection they'll feel! It's like bonding on a deep level, keeping them engaged from beginning to end.

But emotions don't stop there, my friend. Emotionally-driven narratives pack a punch, evoking laughter, joy, sadness, or that jaw-dropping awe. Tap into that emotional goldmine, and your content will be etched into their memories, begging to be shared with the masses.

And here comes the visual feast - visual storytelling. Words alone can tell a story, but visuals, my friend, have the power to bring it to life. From vibrant images to captivating animations to jaw-dropping footage, visuals work their magic, immersing your audience in a viewing experience they won't soon forget.

Now, let's grasp the art of visual communication, that je ne sais quoi that takes your videos from ordinary to extraordinary. Think of it as painting a masterpiece with your camera and editing skills:

Composition is everything. How you arrange the elements within the frame can make or break the visual impact. Embrace concepts like the rule of thirds, leading lines, and framing, and watch as your shots come alive, drawing your audience's eyes right where you want them.

And let there be light! Lighting sets the tone, the mood of your video. You gotta know your way around lighting techniques to set that perfect ambiance. Natural light, artificial lighting - find the right combination and get ready for your videos to shine brighter than ever.

Color grading. Don't underestimate the power of colors. They can spark emotions, create an atmosphere, and make your content truly pop. Play around with color during the editing process, and watch as your videos come alive with the flick of your wrist.

In conclusion, my friend, video content is a true powerhouse when it comes to captivating and engaging audiences. With successful video formats, storytelling techniques that tug at heartstrings, and mastering the art of visual communication, you'll unlock the full potential of video content. So go forth, create powerful videos, and leave a lasting impact on your audience. You've got this!

THE ART OF STORYTELLING

Storytelling, man, it's a real craft. It's like weaving together these different elements to create some mind-blowing narrative that sticks with people, you know? It's not just about throwing info at 'em, it's about creating a whole damn world where imaginations can go wild and emotions can go through the roof. Us content creators, we're like the architects of these worlds, the builders of these strong emotional connections. So, let's get deep into the secrets of crafting stories that grab people by the heart and mind and keep 'em hanging on every word.

At the heart of any killer story are its elements. These bad boys work together, flowing seamlessly, to draw people in and make 'em crave more. And the first element, my friend, is the plot. It's like the backbone of the whole thing, holding everything up. With all its twists and turns, a well-crafted plot keeps people on the edge of their seats, dying to see what happens next. From a simple beginning to a mind-blowing climax, that plot takes 'em on a wild emotional ride that leaves 'em begging for more.

Now, let's talk characters. They bring the story to life, man. They let people relate and connect on a whole different level. It's all about their emotions, their flaws, and their growth - that's what mirrors the human experience, you know? And as content creators, we have the power to shape these characters, to give 'em depth and make 'em real. We gotta create multi-dimensional characters that all kinds of people can relate to, 'cause representation matters, my friend. We gotta make sure everyone feels seen and heard.

But hey, a story can't just rely on plot and characters alone. It needs that little somethin' extra - emotional hooks. Emotions are what keep people hooked, man. Whether it's happiness, sadness, anger, or fear, we gotta tap into those feelings and make 'em hit people right in the gut. That's how we create a story that sticks with 'em long after it's over. We want this story to be more than just a series of events, we want it to be a freakin' experience that people go through with their hearts wide open.

And to do that, we gotta embrace vulnerability, man. It's the key to tapping into those raw, authentic human experiences that make stories compelling. We gotta let people in, share the secrets of our own lives, and build that trust and connection. When we're able to do that, we unlock stories that touch people on a whole different level, my friend. We leave a mark in their hearts and souls that they won't ever forget.

As content creators, we got so many tools and research at our fingertips to up our storytelling game. We gotta study the history of storytelling in different cultures, learn up on all the new techniques - we gotta be hungry to improve, you feel me? Research opens up new ideas, challenges the norm, and helps us push the boundaries of storytelling. And when we pull from different art forms, blend 'em together, we create narratives that blow people's minds and keep 'em on their toes.

But man, storytelling is a never-ending journey. We gotta keep evolving, learning from our successes and failures, and staying open to inspiration from everywhere. We gotta dive deep into literature, cinema, music, art - all the good stuff. They're our best teachers, man. They offer insights and techniques that can take our stories to new heights.

In this book, we're gonna take this journey together, my friend. We're gonna dive into the elements of storytelling, get into the nitty-gritty of character development, and explore those emotional hooks that keep people hooked. We'll analyze, share personal stories, and give you some kickass exercises to unlock the secrets of content creators. It's all about empowering you to craft narratives that hit people right in the feels and make a real impact.

So let your imagination run wild, embrace vulnerability, and let's uncover the art of storytelling

- the beauty, the complexity, all of it. Together, we're gonna shine a light on the path to creating narratives that capture hearts, change minds, and inspire a whole new generation of content creators. Let's do this.

NAVIGATING THE SOCIAL MEDIA LANDSCAPE

So, let's talk about content creation and the incredible power of social media platforms. I mean, seriously, in this digital age, you can't ignore the influence they have on reaching your target audience and building a strong online presence. But here's the thing, social media is constantly changing, and it can be a real challenge to keep up with all the trends and strategies. That's why, in this chapter, I'm going to dive deep into different social media platforms, their unique features, and how you can use them to grow your following and get your content seen by the right people.

First up, let's take a look at the heavy hitters - Instagram and YouTube. Instagram is all about visuals, my friends. You've got photos, videos, and a billion monthly active users hanging out there. It's a massive opportunity to showcase your work and connect with your audience. The cool thing about Instagram is that it's all about aesthetics. They want you to up your game and present your content in the most visually appealing way possible. That means you've got to pay attention to the quality of your photos and videos, as well as the overall look and feel of your feed.

To really make the most of Instagram, you need to know your target audience inside and out. What do they like? What makes them tick? You've got to dig deep and gather insights using analytics tools. Once you've got a handle on who your audience is, you can create content that speaks directly to them - content that they can't resist engaging with.

But it's not just about creating great content. Instagram has all these awesome features and strategies to help you get your stuff out there. Think hashtags, my friend. They're like little magic spells that can help you reach a wider audience. And don't forget about engaging with the community -

commenting, direct messaging, collaborating with other creators. Oh, and Instagram stories and live videos? Those are your behind-the-scenes passes to connect with your followers in real-time.

Now, let's move on to YouTube. This platform has taken the world by storm, folks. It's a video-sharing paradise, and with over 2 billion logged-in monthly users, you've got a massive audience just waiting to devour your content. Unlike other social media platforms, YouTube is all about video. So, if you've got a knack for creating killer videos, this is your playground.

To make the most of YouTube, you've got to focus on creating high-quality videos that bring value to your viewers. That means doing your research and finding out what's trending and what people are searching for. And don't forget to optimize your video titles, descriptions, and tags to boost your discoverability. Oh, and thumbnails? They're like the eye-catching movie posters that get people clicking.

But here's the thing - consistency is your secret

sauce on YouTube. You've got to keep those regular uploads coming and engage with your community through comments and responses. That's how you build up that loyal following and keep 'em coming back for more.

Now, besides Instagram and YouTube, there's a whole world of other social media platforms for you to explore. Facebook, Twitter, TikTok, Pinterest, LinkedIn, Snapchat - they all have their own unique features and target audiences. Take Facebook, for example. You can join groups, create pages, and even run ad campaigns to reach and engage with your people. And Twitter? It's like the spot for real-time updates and quick thoughts.

TikTok, my friends, is the fastest-growing platform out there. It's all about short-form videos and creative storytelling. You've got sound bites, effects, and challenges to play with. It's like a playground for content creators who love to get quirky and shareable.

And let's not forget Pinterest - an image-sharing paradise. You can create boards and share all kinds of visual content that speaks to your niche.Plus, it's got a predominantly female audience, so if that's your target, you're in the right place.

Now, for all you professional peeps out there, LinkedIn is your ticket. It's where you can showcase your work experience, skills, and connect with other professionals in your industry. And lastly, Snapchat. It's all about the ephemeral stuff - snippets of your day, behind-the-scenes peeks, and those limited-time offers that get people excited.

But here's the thing, you've got to know how each platform works and figure out which ones align best with your target audience and content style. By using a combination of platforms, you can expand your reach, engage with a wider audience, and get your content seen by more people. And here's the kicker - stay updated, my friends. It's crucial to stay on top of the latest trends and strategies. That means investing time in research, following influential creators in your niche, and even attending conferences or workshops. The more you know, the more you can adapt and take advantage of new opportunities.

So, to wrap it all up, the social media landscape is a place of endless possibilities for content creators like you. Embrace that power and let your creativity shine on platforms like Instagram, YouTube, and beyond. Create amazing content, engage with your audience, and always stay ahead of the game. And remember, my friends, you've got this!

BUILDING A PERSONAL BRAND

So, you're a content creator, huh? Well, let me tell you, building a killer personal brand is absolutely essential if you want to stand out from the outrageous number of creators out there. Your brand is like your calling card - it shows everyone who you are, what you believe in, and what you bring to the table. Lucky for you, this chapter is all about the essential steps to create a strong personal brand. Grab a seat and get ready to dive in.

First things first, you gotta define your niche. Your audience is the bread and butter of your success, so you better know 'em like the back of your hand. Take the time to research and understand what makes them tick. What are their interests, their needs, their pain points? Once you've got that figured out, you can tailor your content to blow their minds and stand out from the competition.

But hold up, that's not all. You also gotta establish a unique voice. When I say voice, I'm not talking about your singing skills - although, hey, that could be a sweet bonus. I'm talking about the way you express yourself and communicate with your audience. Show 'em who you are, what you're all about. Are you funny? Deep? Authentic? Let that personality shine through and make your content scream, "This is me, folks!"

Now, let's get real - like, super real. Cultivating an authentic online presence is the key to building a killer personal brand. In this digital age, being genuine and transparent is more valuable than gold. So spill the beans, share your story, your ups and downs. Let your audience be a part of your journey as a content creator. Show 'em the real human behind the brand. Trust me, when you do this, it's gonna create a bond so deep, your followers will be all in, no matter what.

Okay, buckle up 'cause I've got a few more strategies to drop on ya. First rule of thumb - consistency. Make sure your brand image, your messaging, your content - they're all consistent across all platforms and channels. People want to see a brand that's solid, not all over the place like a squirrel on caffeine.

Oh, and visuals, my friend, visuals are everything. Invest in some high-quality stuff - photos, videos, graphics that are gonna leave a lasting impression on your audience. Think of it as the cherry on top of your content cake.

Now, collaborations. Find other creators in your niche and team up, my friend. This is like having your own superhero squad. You'll be able to expand your reach and expose yourself to a whole new audience. Cross-promote each other's stuff, work on projects together. It's a win-win situation.

But remember, building a personal brand isn't just about making content and hitting the big time. It's about building a community. Engage with your audience, respond to their comments, their messages, their emails. Show 'em some love and let 'em know that you appreciate their support. That connection is the key to loyalty.

And last but not least, stay on your toes. The online world is constantly changing, my friend. Keep up with new trends and technologies, adapt your brand and content strategy to meet the ever-evolving needs and expectations of your audience. Stay relevant, stay sharp.

So there you have it, my content creator amigo. Building a strong personal brand isn't easy, but with a little effort and a lot of understanding, you'll be killing it in no time. Define your niche, find your voice, and be your authentic self. Stay consistent, invest in quality visuals, engage with your audience, and never stop evolving. Your personal brand is a reflection of you and the value you bring to your audience. Now go out there and own it.

MONETIZATION STRATEGIES

Alright, listen up fellow content creators! We all know the blood, sweat, and tears we pour into our work. We brainstorm, film, edit, and promote like there's no tomorrow. But guess what? I've got some exciting news for you. All that hard work can actually make you some serious cash! That's right, my friends, in this chapter, we're diving deep into the world of monetizing content creation. I'm talking brand partnerships, sponsored content, merchandise sales, and even crowdfunding. Buckle up because I'm about to spill the beans on how to make it rain in this ever-evolving field of content creation.

First up, we've got brand partnerships. Now, this is one hell of a popular and effective way to monetize your content. Picture this - you find a company or brand that aligns perfectly with your values, interests, and niche. You join forces with them and use your influence, creativity, and expertise to create content that promotes their products or services. Cha-ching!

To attract these brand partnerships, you've gotta build a strong online presence, continuously churn out high-quality content, and engage with your audience like a pro. Companies are all about creators with a loyal and engaged following because they know you can market their stuff to a targeted audience like nobody's business.

But here's the thing, when you dive into a brand partnership, you gotta make sure you negotiate fair compensation for your work. That could be a flat fee, a cut of the sales you generate, or even free goodies. Oh, and most importantly, it has to feel real and authentic, both for you and your audience. Trust is everything, people!

Moving on to sponsored content. This is kinda like brand partnerships, but it's more of a one-time gig. You collaborate with companies to create content that promotes their products or services. Again, authenticity is key here. You gotta make sure the collaboration aligns with your values and interests. Your audience trusts your recommendations, so you gotta be genuine when you're pushing products or services their way. Oh, and don't forget to disclose those sponsored collaborations. Transparency is the name of the game, my friends!

Now, let's talk merchandise sales. We all love rocking some swag, right? Well, selling merchandise is a fantastic way to monetize your content creation. You can slap your brand on some sick apparel, accessories, or even digital products like e-books or exclusive content. But here's the deal - you gotta build a strong personal brand first. You need that dedicated fanbase who's all about what you're putting out there. You want them to buy your stuff because they feel connected to your content and your values. And hey, make sure your designs and products are top-notch. Customer satisfaction is key for repeat purchases, my friends.

Last but not least, we've got crowdfunding. This one's for all you creators with big dreams and bold ideas. Crowdfunding platforms like Kickstarter, Patreon, or GoFundMe allow you to raise funds directly from your audience. You pitch your projects, and your viewers can shower you with financial support. It works even better if you've got a passionate fanbase that's dying to see you succeed. Offer some cool rewards or exclusive access to certain content, and you'll have them lining up to contribute.

But hold up, there's more! I've got some killer tips for you to achieve financial success as a content creator. First, diversify your income streams. Don't put all your eggs in one basket. Explore different avenues and make sure you've got multiple money-makers to cushion any financial uncertainties.

Next, invest in yourself and your skills. You've gotta stay ahead of the game as content creation evolves. Take courses, attend workshops, and learn new skills so you can keep delivering that unique value to your audience.

And hey, don't forget to track and analyze your data. Knowing your audience, their engagement, and your revenue sources is vital for making smart decisions. Use analytics tools and keep an eye on your progress so you can optimize your money-making strategies.

Now, it's important to remember that success

takes time and persistence. Overnight fame is a rare gem, so stay committed to your craft and keep pushing forward even when things get tough.

Oh, and here's a golden nugget - network and collaborate with other creators. This can expand your audience reach, teach you heaps from their experiences, and maybe even open doors to exciting partnerships and brand collaborations.

In conclusion, my fellow content creators, monetizing your work is a strategic game. It's all about finding that perfect mix of brand partnerships, sponsored content, merchandise sales, and crowdfunding that aligns with your content, your values, and your audience. So go out there, implement these killer strategies, and pave your way to the sweet sweet land of financial success. It's time to make that content creation dream a reality!

The Dark Side of Content Creation

THE PSYCHOLOGICAL TOLL

Let me tell you something about online criticism, my friend. When you put your heart and soul into creating something and upload it to the vast digital world, you expose yourself to the opinions of an ever-growing audience. And let me tell you, people on the internet can be brutal. They hide behind their screens, dropping thoughts and judgments without a care for how it might affect your mental wellbeing. It's like a battlefield out there, and many content creators end up grappling with the emotional fallout of this unfiltered feedback.

But here's the thing, online criticism cuts both ways. On one hand, it can be a driving force, motivating us to improve and grow as artists. Constructive feedback, my friend, can be a game-changer. It gives us valuable insights that help us sharpen our craft and take it to new levels. But sometimes, that line between constructive criticism and outright vitriol blurs, leaving us vulnerable, doubting our own worth. It's important to develop a thick skin, to know that not all criticism defines us. Filtering out the negativity and focusing on the constructive bits becomes crucial in preserving our sanity.

Now, let me tell you about the devil called comparison syndrome. In this age of social media, comparison is like a devil lurking behind every corner. We're bombarded with perfectly curated content, beautiful lives, and seemingly flawless talents. It's way too easy to fall into the trap of comparing ourselves, measuring our worth against those unachievable standards. But listen closely, my friend. We are unique individuals with our own creative voices. Embrace your individuality, nurture your own journey, and remember that success isn't just about numbers or popularity. Value your personal growth, find satisfaction in your own creative path, and shield yourself from the poisonous effects of comparison syndrome.

Ah, validation, my dear friend. The quest for validation is what keeps so many content creators awake at night. We crave positive feedback, recognition, to know that our work matters. And let me tell you, it can be a blessing and a curse. Positive vibes fuel our creativity, give us wings to soar, and the confidence to keep going. But here's the catch, relying too heavily on external validation can chip away at our self-worth. It creates a never-ending thirst for approval that can never be fully quenched.

To break free from this never-ending quest, we need to cultivate self-acceptance and self-confidence. Realize that our worth as creators isn't solely based on what others think. Seek validation from within, find joy in the process of creation, and focus on the impact our content has on ourselves and those who connect with it. That sense of fulfillment is far more meaningful than any external praise.

Now, my friend, let me share some strategies to help content creators navigate these turbulent waters. Self-care should always be a priority. Take care of your mental and emotional wellbeing, my friend. Engage in activities that relax your mind, find your zen through mindfulness exercises, move your body with physical exercise, and explore creative outlets unrelated to your content creation. All of this will give you a much-needed break from the pressures and expectations you place upon yourself.

Building a support network is vital. Surround yourself with like-minded individuals who understand the challenges you face. They offer validation, empathy, and guidance. Share your experiences, collaborate, and support each other—it's like a lifeline in this seemingly solitary journey.

And lastly, establish boundaries in the digital realm. Create a clear separation between work and personal life. Enforce healthy usage of social media platforms, so your mental wellbeing isn't constantly on display, susceptible to comparison and criticism. Protect yourself, my friend.

So, in conclusion, content creation can be a hell of a ride. You navigate the treacherous waters of online criticism, comparison syndrome, and the never-ending thirst for validation. But by understanding these challenges and implementing coping mechanisms, we empower ourselves to maintain our mental wellbeing, foster our creativity, and continue to share our untold secrets with the world. Trust me, my friend, you've got this.

THE PRICE OF FAME

I gotta admit, fame is a real tricky beast. It's like this double-edged sword, ya know? On one side, you get all this recognition and success, but man, on the other side, there's a heavy price you gotta pay. As content creators, we're always tryin' to juggle our public and private lives. And let me tell ya, it ain't easy.

When we first start out on this journey, it's all innocent and fueled by passion. We just wanna share our creativity with the world and connect with people. But as our following grows, so do the demands and expectations. The line between our personal and public lives starts to blur, and suddenly, everything we do and say gets scrutinized.

We used to just do what we loved, ya know? It was our hobby, a way to express ourselves. But now? It's a freakin' business. And everyone's watching, taking notes. Our personal lives become like public property, and it feels like a million strangers are dissecting every damn move we make.

Gotta make sacrifices if you wanna make it big. Time with loved ones, that used to be priceless, becomes a rare commodity. The pressure to create more and better content leaves little room for personal relationships. We find ourselves choosing deadlines over quality time with partners, friends, and family. It's a tough choice, but when you're chasin' success, it's one you gotta make.

But here's the thing - fame don't just stay on social media. Nah, it follows us everywhere. We're constantly under the watchful eye of the public. Every slip-up and moment of vulnerability gets captured and shared. It's like we can't even separate our public persona from our real selves anymore. We're trapped behind these expectations that fans have of us.

And let me tell ya, it's our relationships that take the biggest hit. The demands of this career don't leave much time for personal connections. Our partners, who used to be our rocks, start feelin' neglected. We get so wrapped up in keepin' up appearances that we accidentally push away the people who matter most to us.

And it doesn't stop there. Our relationships become fuel for the rumor mill. People love gossip, and when you're famous, it's like they can't get enough. We're constantly dealing with rumors and speculation that strain even the strongest of bonds. Trust gets shattered, and the intrusion caused by our fame leaves a mark on our personal lives forever.

But lemme tell ya, the toll fame takes on our mental health is no joke. The pressure to stay on top and relevant can mess with your head big time. It's this never-ending cycle of anxiety and self-doubt. Our worth gets measured by the number of likes, views, and shares we get. And what used to bring us joy and fulfillment can easily turn into a source of stress.

As content creators, we need to recognize the price of fame. We gotta set boundaries to protect our personal lives from the prying eyes of the public. Our relationships need to be a priority, even in the chaos of our careers. And most importantly, we gotta take care of ourselves and our mental health. Fame should be a part of our lives, not our whole lives.

Yeah, the cost of fame is high, my friends. But it's up to us to decide if it's worth it. We gotta navigate the blurred lines, sacrifices, and invasion of privacy with resilience and self-awareness. Only then can we truly embrace the opportunities and rewards that fame brings, without sacrificin' our happiness and relationships.

So stay tuned, 'cause we're just gettin' started. There's so much more to uncover in this crazy world of content creators.

OVERCOMING BURNOUT

Man, let me tell you, being a content creator is like being in an epic race against time. We're constantly under pressure to churn out captivating content day in and day out. It can get overwhelming, bro. We push ourselves to meet deadlines, respond to comments, engage with our audience, and stay relevant in this ever-changing digital game. It's a fast-paced, demanding world out there, and if we ain't careful, burnout can sneak up on us real quick.

But here's the thing, my friend. We gotta take a breather every now and then. We gotta replenish our own well-being before it runs dry. In this chapter, I'm gonna spill the beans and share some practical strategies and self-care techniques that have saved my ass from burnout, helped me manage stress, and kept me from losing my sanity in this crazy content creation game.

First things first, we gotta learn to recognize the signs of burnout before it completely engulfs us. Burnout ain't no joke, man. It comes in different forms – physical, emotional, and mental exhaustion. It's like feeling drained 24/7, being irritated with the world, and losing all motivation. We can't just brush it off as mere fatigue, my dude. Burnout can mess us up real good, both physically and mentally. Once you realize you're experiencing burnout, you gotta take action, man.

Now, one of the most effective weapons against burnout is setting boundaries. I know it can be tough when our work is intertwined with our personal lives, but trust me, drawing that line is crucial for staying sane. Set specific working hours, find yourself a dedicated workspace, and create a routine that includes time to kick back, relax, and do stuff that brings you joy.

But hey, boundaries alone ain't gonna cut it. We gotta take care of ourselves, man. As content creators, we get so wrapped up in our work that we forget to take care of our own well-being. Self-care, my friend, it's the name of the game. It's not just about physical health, it's about keeping our minds and emotions in check too. Whether it's zoning out with some meditation or yoga, getting lost in a creative hobby, or just chilling with the people we love, we gotta invest in ourselves. That's how we bring our A-game to the content we create.

Managing stress, bro, that's another beast we gotta wrangle. Stress can weigh us down and make us doubt ourselves, man. It's crucial to identify the sources of stress and learn some coping mechanisms that work for us. Take a deep breath, jot your thoughts down, or go bust a move. And don't forget, it's okay to prioritize tasks, ask for help when you need it, and say "no" when your workload is just too damn much. Control your stress levels, my dude. Don't let that burnout monster take over your life.

And you know what, we can't do this alone.

We gotta build ourselves a supportive network. We spend so much time locked away in our little content creation caves, it's easy to feel isolated. But connecting with others who get our struggle, man, that's gold. Hit up industry events, join online communities, or even team up with fellow content creators. Surrounding ourselves with people who've been through the same battles, who share their experiences and insights, that's how we find solace. We're not alone, my friend. We're in this together.

Lastly, and I can't stress this enough, we gotta remember we're humans, not machines. We got limits, man. It's okay to take breaks, step back, and reset. I know it's tempting to stay in the hustle mindset and forget about ourselves, but that ain't gonna end well. So, let's be smart – prioritize self-care, set those boundaries, manage that stress, build that network – and keep creating content that makes a real impact.

To wrap it all up, remember this – the content creation world can chew us up and spit us out if we don't take care of ourselves. But with these practical strategies and self-care techniques, we'll be armed and ready to fight burnout, manage stress, and keep that work-life balance in check.

Taking care of ourselves ain't just for our well-being, bro. It's also for the quality of the content we create. So let's make it happen, my friend.

Prioritize self-care, set them boundaries, manage that stress, build that network, and let's keep slaying this content creation game.

NAVIGATING ONLINE HARASSMENT

So, picture this, my fellow content creators. We put our heart and soul into our work, striving to create content that grabs our audience's attention and sparks meaningful conversations. But there's this dark side to the digital universe - online harassment. It's like this relentless force that's out to mess with our heads and mess up our mental well-being. In this chapter, we're plunging straight into the belly of the beast. We'll dig deep into the impact online harassment has on our mental health, check out the legal options we have, and arm ourselves with some self-protection tips.

Let's start with the mental health part. Online harassment has this sneaky way of worming into every nook and cranny of our lives. It messes with our thoughts and fills our minds with negativity. Those hate-filled comments, threats, and personal attacks? They eat away at our self-worth, making us feel exposed and vulnerable. We've got to acknowledge the toll this takes on our mental health if we're gonna tackle it head-on.

Research is slapping us in the face with some hard facts. It shows that online harassment can mess with our mental health big time. It can pump up our anxiety, make our depression worse, and mess with other mental health stuff we might already be dealing with. The fear that hangs over us, never knowing when or where the next attack will come from, it cranks up our stress levels. And that has a serious impact on our overall well-being. We're talking sleep problems, messed-up appetites, and pulling away from people who matter in our lives. All signs that online harassment is gnawing at our mental health.

Now, let's dive into the legal side of things. When we're faced with online harassment, we gotta arm ourselves with knowledge about the legal options we have. Sure, the laws might be different from one country to another, but there are some principles we can all cling to. Most places have laws that cover cyberbullying, and that's a good starting point. We need to get familiar with these laws, gather evidence, and maybe even tap into some legal advice. It's about the harassers being held accountable and finding some solace in the legal system.

But hey, let's keep it real. Navigating the legal process can be a nightmare. It's time-consuming, intimidating, and sometimes, just plain scary. And us content creators, we're not always so eager to take on that legal beast. We worry about more retaliation or the financial strain it might bring. That's when we gotta lean on the organizations and communities that fight this crap all the time. They've got our backs, offering support, resources, and a sense of united strength. We're not alone in this battle, my friends.

Okay, now for some self-protection tips. We might not be able to wipe out online harassment entirely, but we sure as heck can make it a little harder for those harassers to get us. First up, let's surround ourselves with a supportive network. We need a crew of creators who get it, who know what it's like to deal with this junk. They'll give us emotional support and wicked advice to navigate the online harassment storms.

And how about some digital hygiene? We've gotta stay clean and safe, my friends. Regularly checking those privacy settings, making sure we're not leaking personal info left and right. We gotta be savvy about who we accept as online pals and who gives us the creeps. By keeping our guard up, we lower the chances of being targeted by those harassers.

And let's not forget about the tech tools that can save our sanity. The social media platforms we use often have these nifty moderation options. We need to learn how to use them to our advantage. Filtering out the harmful and offensive stuff is key, my friends. Don't let it get to you.

Now, listen up. We need to be bold and take action when needed. If harassment strikes, we report it, plain and simple. The platform needs to know what's going on. And then we block or mute those accounts that are throwing the shade. We cut off that direct line of communication. Ain't nobody got time for their toxic nonsense.

Last but not least, we gotta take care of ourselves. Seriously, self-care is crucial when faced with online harassment. It's about making ourselves a priority. Doing things that bring us joy and help us unwind from all the stress. And it's about surrounding ourselves with good vibes, countering all the negativity that comes with online harassment.

We're reaching the end now, my fellow content creators. Online harassment is this scary, alarming issue we can't ignore. It messes with our mental health and threatens our creative safe space. But we're fighters, aren't we? We know that to navigate this mess, we gotta first understand how it messes with us. We gotta check out the legal paths we can take and arm ourselves with some self-protection knowledge. Together, we're stronger. And together, we'll create a brighter digital future, one that's free from online harassment.

AUTHENTICITY VS. EXPECTATIONS

I gotta tell ya, being a content creator is like walking on a tightrope, trying to balance being yourself with meeting the expectations of your audience. It's a constant struggle that I've found myself in time and time again. On one hand, I want to stay true to my own voice and style, but on the other hand, I also want to give my viewers what they want. It's like a tug of war, and in this chapter, we're gonna dive deep into this whole battle and see how content creators navigate through this crazy world of modern media.

First off, we gotta talk about how much power content creators actually have in today's society. I mean, with social media blowing up, anyone can become a star overnight with just a camera and an internet connection. But fame ain't all sunshine and rainbows, my friends. It comes with its own set of challenges and pressures.

Authenticity is the name of the game for us content creators. When we're real and genuine, it creates this special connection with our audience. It's like they can feel it in their bones, you know? And that connection is what keeps 'em coming back for more. They trust us, they're loyal to us, all because we give 'em that authenticity. It's like magic.

But here's the thing, as we get more popular, the weight of expectations gets heavier and heavier. Our audience, God bless 'em, they want consistency, they want entertainment, and sometimes that means we gotta bend to their will. And that's where things get a little tricky. 'Cause when we start conforming to all those demands, we risk losing our authenticity, our true selves. It's like a never-ending battle of what's real versus what's desired. And let me tell ya, it takes some serious soul searching to navigate through this crazy terrain.

Now, here's the million-dollar question: Is success in content creation all about authenticity or giving in to audience expectations? Can we strike a balance between the two? After my fair share of experience, I've come to realize that the secret sauce lies in finding your own unique voice and sticking to it, while still keeping your audience's desires in mind.

But man, the fear of losing our authenticity is a force to be reckoned with. We're constantly on edge, constantly worried that by trying to meet audience expectations, we might compromise who we really are. It's like a rollercoaster ride, my friends. Scary as hell, but also thrilling. It takes a whole lot of self-awareness and reflection to navigate this treacherous path.

But here's the silver lining: being authentic doesn't mean we gotta stay stagnant. It's about embracing who we are while also growing as artists. We gotta find that sweet spot where we're true to ourselves, but also open to change and evolve. It's like strutting through life with our heads held high, knowing who we are but being willing to take risks.

To truly understand the struggle between authenticity and expectations, I did my homework. I talked to my fellow content creators, and boy, did I learn a thing or two. Let me tell you about Sarah, this beauty influencer who had a huge following. She built her empire by promoting natural beauty and self-acceptance, but as her popularity skyrocketed, her viewers started begging for more makeup tutorials. Talk about a tough spot, right? Sarah found herself drifting away from her original message, trapped in a web of expectations.

But guess what? Sarah, bless her soul, she found a way to incorporate the makeup tutorials without sacrificing who she truly was. She managed to meet her audience's expectations while staying authentic to herself. And you know what? That made her shine even brighter.

The battle between authenticity and expectations is a never-ending saga for content creators. The pressure to conform for success is real, and many fall into the trap of losing themselves in the pursuit of fame and fortune. But those who have the strength to stay true to themselves while also adapting to their audience's desires, those are the ones who leave their mark in this crazy world of content creation.

As I reflect on my own journey, I realize there's no one-size-fits-all solution to this dilemma. Every creator has to find their own balance between authenticity and meeting audience expectations. It takes a deep understanding of who we are and who our audience is, and the guts to take risks and pave our own damn path.

In the end, it all comes down to this ongoing dance between authenticity and expectations. It's a constant battle, my friends, one that requires us to look deep within, to grow, to adapt, and to reflect. But trust me when I say this: by embracing the challenge and finding our own unique voice, we can break free from the chains of conformity and leave a lasting impact on the world of media. Now that's something worth fighting for, don't ya think?

CHAPTER 4

Mastering Content Creation Techniques

THE ART OF VIDEO EDITING

Alright, folks, listen up. If you're looking to dive into the exciting world of video editing, you've got to wade through a sea of software options. And let me tell you, the choice you make can make or break your final masterpiece. We're talking about Adobe Premiere Pro, Final Cut Pro, and DaVinci Resolve, just to name a few.

For me, my go-to weapon of choice is none other than Adobe Premiere Pro. It's like a best friend that never fails me, ya know? With its straightforward interface and an arsenal of editing tools, it's the perfect partner in crime to bring my creative ideas to life. Now, Final Cut Pro, that one's a fan-favorite among all you Mac users out there. It seamlessly integrates with Apple's whole shindig, and its timeline-based editing system is as smooth as butter. And then there's DaVinci Resolve, that little gem that started out as a color grading software and grew into a full-blown editing powerhouse. It's got all the bells and whistles, from advanced editing capabilities to loads of visual effects.

But hold up, software choice is just the beginning. Now it's time to dive deep into the techniques that turn video editing into an art form. Let's talk transitions, my friends. You want your shots to flow together like a river, so those seamless transitions are key. Picture this: cuts, fades, dissolves, and wipes leading the way.

Cuts, they're like the OG of transitions. One shot abruptly replaces the other — talk about making a statement. Fades, they're more sneaky. You gradually blend two shots together, playing with the opacity to give that smooth blend. Dissolves, they take it up a notch. They're like fades, but instead of gradually replacing a shot, they create this magical crossfade effect. And then wipes, they're all about bringing out the big guns. Picture a line or shape moving across the screen, taking you from one shot to the next.

Just like a cherry on top, visual effects are essential for taking your videos to a whole new level. They have this crazy superpower to turn plain footage into mind-blowing awesomeness. We're talking explosions, muzzle flashes, jaw-dropping motion graphics, and mind-boggling 3D animations. And let me tell you, achieving those visual effects takes a combo of crazy techniques and specialized software. Think Adobe After Effects or Blackmagic Fusion – they're like the secret weapons in a content creator's toolbox. With all the tools and features they offer, there's no limit to what you can dream up.

And let's not forget those captivating montages – that's where the real magic happens. They're like a carefully crafted puzzle of shots and images that tell a story or evoke pure emotion. Montages can speed up time, build suspense, or just showcase stunning moments. It's all about picking the right shots and arranging them in a way that flows like honey. The rhythm and timing of the edits are what set the pace and tone – you can make hearts race, bring tears to eyes, or leave people in awe.

I don't know about you, but I'm constantly blown away by the infinite possibilities of video editing. It's like a beautiful dance between technical know-how and unleashing your creative genius. It's a playground where software becomes your trusty sidekick, and transitions and effects groove to the beat of your imagination. Each montage is a masterpiece waiting to be discovered. So, buckle up, my friends, because we're about to unlock the secrets of the content creators and venture into a world of pure awesomeness.

CAPTIVATING AUDIO PRODUCTION

Alright, folks, let's dive into the wild world of content creation. It's a crazy-fast industry where grabbing your audience's attention is like trying to catch a unicorn - super tough. But fear not, my fellow creators, because I've discovered a secret weapon that can really take your projects to the next level. And that, my friends, is killer audio production.

Now, I may just be a humble content creator, but I've learned a thing or two about the power of audio quality. So, in this chapter, I'm gonna spill all the beans on how you can achieve that professional-grade audio that'll make your audience's ears prick up in delight. You ready?

First things first, let's talk about microphone selection. This is the foundation of great audio, my friends. With so many options out there, it can feel like wading through a swamp of choices. But fear not, champs! I'll guide you through the key factors to consider.

See, each microphone has its own magical powers that work best in different situations. Take dynamic mics like the Shure SM7B, for example. These babies are amazing at cutting out background noise and giving your voice that warm, velvety tone. Perfect for podcasts and voice-overs, if you ask me. Then there are condenser mics, like the Neumann U87, which are like audio wizards. They capture every little sound detail, making them perfect for musical recordings or high-quality vocals.

Alright, now that we've got the right mic in hand, it's time to work some sound editing magic. This step is all about polishing your audio, my friends. You wanna make sure there are no un-wanted noises or imperfections distracting your audience from your genius. Lucky for you, I've gathered a bunch of tips and tricks to help you master the art of sound editing.

You gotta get cozy with programs like Adobe Audition or Audacity. These bad boys let you do all the cool stuff, like removing pesky background noise, adjusting audio levels, and making your overall sound quality shine like a diamond. And don't forget about equalization (EQ) - it's like a magic spell for fine-tuning frequencies and making your audio pop with depth and clarity. Oh, and compression! Can't forget about that one. It's like a superhero that tames the dynamic range and keeps your audio volume consistent throughout.

Now, let's talk about voice modulation. Your voice is way more than just a bunch of words, my friends. It's an instrument that can weave emotions, stir up empathy, and totally captivate your audience. So, if you wanna hit 'em right in the feels, you gotta master the art of voice modulation.

Start by playing around with pacing and intonation. Trust me, finding that sweet spot will keep your audience hanging on to your every word. Experimenting with pitch and volume can amp up the excitement and make your listeners sit up and take notice. And don't be afraid to emphasize certain words or toss in a well-placed pause here and there. These little tricks can take your voice from "meh" to "whoa" in no time.

Now, let's take a little journey into the world of immersive soundscapes. Strap on your adventure boots, my friends, 'cause we're about to transport your audience to new dimensions. Adding immersive soundscapes can be a game-changer, whether you're creating a podcast, video, or even a virtual reality experience. It's the difference between having a passive audience and having them completely engaged and hooked.

So, how do you create these epic soundscapes? Pay attention to the atmosphere, my friends. Don't be afraid to sprinkle in the gentle rustling of leaves, the bustling sounds of a city, or the crashing of waves. These subtle touches add depth and whisk your audience right into the heart of the scene. And let's not forget about sound effects and music! They're like the secret sauce that sets the mood and adds that emotional punch to your content. Get creative with different combos, making sure that every audio element seamlessly blends with your visuals and storytelling.

Okay, now let's take a little field trip to a real-life example of captivating audio production - a kick-ass podcast called "Into the Abyss." Oh man, this true crime thriller has captivated audiences with its top-notch audio quality and gripping stories. Let's break it down and see how they nailed it.

First off, microphone selection was key for "Into the Abyss." They went with the Shure SM7B, which really captured host Sarah Thompson's voice with amazing clarity. It blocked out any distracting background noise and added a touch of authenticity that really hit home with the listeners. Then there's the sound editing. Sarah worked her magic with Adobe Audition, meticulously cleaning up any pesky background noise and making sure the audio levels were perfecto. EQ and compression were her secret weapons, enhancing the clarity and impact of her voice. Listeners were completely immersed in the details of each case.

Sarah's vocal expertise was the icing on the cake. She knew how to modulate her voice like a boss, taking her audience along on a rollercoaster ride of emotions. Her pacing, intonation, and emphasis were spot-on, keeping her listeners on the edge of their seats.

Lastly, Sarah was the queen of creating immersive soundscapes. She carefully crafted a sonic world that transported her audience right into the heart of each crime. With atmospheric sounds, sound effects, and haunting music, listeners felt like they were standing right next to the victims, detectives, and suspects. It was an audio experience they couldn't get enough of.

So, my fellow content creators, remember this: nailing that professional-grade audio quality is an art form. Whether it's picking the right microphone, mastering sound editing, playing with voice modulation, or creating mind-blowing soundscapes, these are the tools that'll captivate your audience like never before. Let your audio be the secret weapon that takes your content to new heights and leaves the world begging for more.

DESIGNING EYE-CATCHING GRAPHICS

Man, you know what really sets my soul on fire? Designing eye-catching graphics. I mean, I live for this stuff. As a content creator, I've come to understand just how important it is to create visuals that grab my audience's attention and leave them begging for more. And in this chapter, I'm about to spill some serious knowledge on graphic design principles, color theory, typography, and the whole shebang. Get ready to have your mind blown.

Let's start with the basics, my friend. Graphic design principles are the bread and butter of creating visuals that are easy on the eyes. You gotta have balance, dude. It's like finding the perfect sweet spot between all the elements in your design. You throw in some strategic placement of images and text, and boom, you've got a visually pleasing composition that'll blow minds left and right.

But wait, there's more. Let's talk contrast. If you want your graphics to jump out and grab attention, you gotta create contrast between different elements. Think contrasting colors, sizes, and typography styles that make people go, "Whoa, dude, that's intense!" It's all about visual interest and getting those important elements to shine bright like a diamond.

Now, don't even get me started on alignment. It's like the secret sauce for a clean and organized design. When your elements are all aligned, like a boss, along a grid or some visual cues, you end up with a design that screams "I'm a professional, baby!" Yeah, that's the kind of vibe you wanna go for.

And last but not least, hierarchy. It's like having a boss that tells you what's important and what's not. Establishing a clear hierarchy in your design helps guide people's eyeballs to the most important bits. You can play around with sizes, colors, and placement to make sure the important stuff is front and center. It's like giving people a roadmap to navigate your design, man.

Now, let's dive into the magical world of color theory. Brace yourself, because colors can seriously mess with your emotions and set the vibe for your visuals. It's like a superpower. First things first, there's this thing called a color wheel. It's like a circle that brings together all the colors in the universe and helps us understand their relationships. And you know what? We got primary colors, secondary colors (which are created by mixing primary colors), and even tertiary colors (which are like the lovechild of primary and secondary colors).

But it doesn't stop there. Color harmony is where the real magic happens. When you create harmonious color schemes, it's like watching a symphony unfold before your eyes. Complementary colors (opposites on the color wheel), analogous colors (neighbors on the wheel), and monochromatic colors (different shades of the same color) all play a role in creating visuals that are harmonious and delightful. It's like creating a masterpiece that leaves people in awe, man.

Oh, and let's not forget about the emotional impact of colors. Different colors can seriously mess with your mood, dude. Warm colors like red and orange give you a burst of energy, while cool colors like blue and green bring a sense of calm and tranquility. It's like having a secret weapon to convey just the right vibe in your visuals. Choose your colors wisely, my friend, and watch the magic happen.

Moving on to the art of typography. This is

where we make words look sexy, bro. Picking the right font is like finding the perfect outfit for a hot date. You gotta consider the overall style and tone of your content and choose fonts that align with your brand image. And hey, why not throw in some font combinations just to keep things interesting? Let your creativity run wild, man.

But here's the thing. Readability is key. You don't want people squinting and scratching their heads trying to decipher your genius words. Keep the legibility game strong by considering factors like font size, line spacing, and letter spacing. You want your words to flow like a smooth jazz melody, bro.

And let's not forget about hierarchy and emphasis. This is how you guide people through your design, like a true master. Headings, subheadings, body text – they all deserve their moment in the spotlight. Experiment with different fonts weights, sizes, and styles to create emphasis and draw attention to those oh-so-important tidbits. It's like putting a spotlight on the stars of your show, man.

Alright, now it's time to put all this knowledge into action and create some jaw-dropping visuals. Let's start with thumbnails. These bad boys are like the first impression you make on your audience. They gotta be visually captivating and make people stop dead in their tracks. Use contrasting colors, bold typography, and killer images that scream "Click me, bro!" You want people rushing to hit that play button like it's Black Friday.

And channel banners, man. These are like the face of your brand. Don't be shy – show 'em what you got. Incorporate your logo, brand colors, and some epic imagery that represents who you are. Keep it simple, keep it clean, and let it reflect your brand's identity. It's like pulling off a crisp, fresh outfit that turns heads on the catwalk.

And last but not least, social media graphics. These babies are all about consistency. You want your brand identity to shine through on every platform. So, use the same colors, typography styles, and imagery across the board. That way, people can spot your content from a mile away, and they'll know it's the bomb. Mix it up with different formats and layouts that stand out in the noise of social media. It's like being the life of the party, dude.

So, armed with these insights, go forth, my friend. Experiment, explore your creativity, and create visuals that leave a lasting impression on your audience. Because let me tell you, a visually captivating design can work wonders. Don't underestimate the power of art, my dude.

CONTENT PLANNING AND ORGANIZATION

Alright, so let's talk about content planning. You know, one of the first things I do is create this badass editorial calendar. It's like a roadmap that tells me what topics to cover, how and when to release my content. Trust me, it's a game-changer.

I usually plan this bad boy on a monthly basis. It gives me the perfect bird's-eye view of what I gotta create and when I gotta drop it. Keeps me on track and helps me stay relevant and in the game.

Now, to make sure my calendar is on point, I start with topic research. Gotta identify the trends that are rocking my niche and see what my target audience is all about. I'm digging into stuff like keyword research, social media listening, and industry reports. It's like being a detective, uncovering the gems that my audience wants to see.

Once I've gathered all this intel, it's time to dive into audience analysis. I gotta know my peeps inside out to create content that makes them go, "Hell yeah, this speaks to me!" So, I'm taking surveys, checking social media analytics, and website metrics to figure out who they are and what makes 'em tick. I wanna make content that's as personalized as possible.

Now, all this juicy information goes into my editorial calendar. I slot in the topics for each juicy day, making sure it all lines up nicely. But hey, I ain't rigid, I leave room for a little flex in case something changes last minute.

And you know what? Timing is everything. So

optimizing the release schedule is just as crucial. Gotta know when my audience is most active, taking into account different time zones and stuff. I wanna hit 'em when they're most likely to engage and share my content. It's like a well-orchestrated dance, getting the timing just right.

So bottom line, this content planning stuff is a total game-changer. It keeps me focused, organized, and achieving maximum impact with my content. Plus, it has upped my creative game like whoa. You gotta give it a shot, my friend. Embrace the power of planning and organization, and watch your creativity soar. Trust me, it's worth it.

CRAFTING COMPELLING STORIES

Introduction: The Essence of Storytelling

Man, there's something truly magical about spinning tales that can hook people's hearts and minds. I mean, think about it - throughout history, stories have shaped entire civilizations, sparked rebellions, and kept generations entertained. And that magic transcends into the world of content creation, my friends. When we embrace the power of storytelling, we're able to connect with people on a whole 'nother level, way beyond just spewing out information.

Exploring Narrative Structures

Now, let's talk about what makes a story so dang good. It all comes down to having a solid narrative structure that's gonna grab your audience by the collar and not let go. See, understanding these structures gives us content creators the tools to finesse our craft and create stories that hit people right in the feels. You've got your classic three-act structure, sure, but don't be afraid to go wild with more experimental forms. The possibilities are endless, my friends. Each structure presents a unique opportunity to engage our audience, tickle their curiosity, and keep 'em hooked.

Now, let's take a trip down what I like to call the Hero's Journey. It's a timeless structure that takes us on a wild ride with a main character, showing us their growth, their ability to bounce back, and their ultimate triumph over adversity. Trust me, this structure taps right into our universal craving for personal growth and inspires us to be the heroes of our own lives.

Character Arcs: Breathing Life into Characters

But hold up a sec, my dudes and dudettes. We can't forget about the characters that make our stories come alive. Gotta give 'em that special somethin' to make 'em memorable, you know? Characters that hit home with your audience, that make 'em feel something deep in their guts. It's all about that connection between storyteller and audience, and memorable characters make that bond unbreakable.

To create those unforgettable characters, we gotta dive deep into their minds, their motivations, their fears, and their dreams. Let's face it - these characters gotta face some inner demons, go through transformational experiences, and show their true colors. By letting 'em grow, we're makin' these stories reflect real life, and that's 'bout as authentic as it gets. Your viewers will feel that connection in their very souls, my friend.

The Art of Tension and Resolution

Alright, buckle up 'cause we're about to take a ride on the plot development rollercoaster. A captivating plot is all about messin' with your audience's emotions, keepin' 'em on the edge of their seats 'til the very end. We're talkin' twists, turns, and unexpected bombshells, my amigos. It's through conflict, rising action, and resolution that we're able to stir up a mix of emotions in our audience.

And let's not forget the power of suspense, my peeps. By buildin' up that tension like nobody's business, we're gonna have 'em hooked and begging for more. Each plot point has gotta be crafted with care, revealin' just enough to keep 'em invested but leavin' 'em curious as all get out. It's all about that fine line between showin' and holdin' back. Trust me, you'll take 'em on a wild ride that'll leave 'em beggin' for another round.

Techniques to Evoke Emotions in Viewers

Now, let me give you a crash course in hitting 'em right in the feels. Emotions, my friends, are what make storytelling so powerful. They're the bridge that connects us content creators to our audience in a way that no amount of information can. When we tap into those raw, primal emotions, we're creating content that'll stick with 'em forever.

So, here are a few techniques to get those tears flowin' and those hearts racin':

First up, we got "show, don't tell." Forget about just tellin' your audience how your characters feel. Show 'em instead. Paint a vivid picture with your words, describe how their faces look, their body language, and let their dialogue speak for 'em. Trust me, your audience will feel like they're right there in the story.

Next, let's dive into symbolism. This little trick adds some serious depth to your storytelling. It lets your audience interpret meaning beyond what's right on the surface. So, weave symbols into your narratives like they're threads in a rich tapestry. It'll evoke emotions on a whole other level, my pals.

And now, we're gonna talk about sound and music. These bad boys have a way of tugging at our heartstrings. So, be picky about the soundscapes and the music you choose to accompany your content. Let 'em work their magic and amplify the emotional oomph of your story.

Last but not least, let's get real, my friends. Share some vulnerable moments, some personal stories straight from the heart. Being authentic is gonna create that emotional bond between you and your viewers. They'll feel like they're connectin' with a real human being, and that creates trust. Trust me, you won't find a stronger connection anywhere else.

Unleashing Your Creative Potential

So, my fellow storytellers, here's the deal. Crafting stories is an art form that lets us unlock our creative potential like nobody's business. By playin' around with narrative structures, character arcs, plot development, and emotional techniques, we're creating content that's gonna light up the world. Embrace that storytelling power and let your imagination soar, my friends. Leave your mark on the content creation landscape with stories that are gonna keep 'em coming back for more. Step out of the ordinary, and you'll form a bond with your viewers that's unbreakable. Go on now, unleash that creative beast within you. The world is waitin' for your untold secrets.

CHAPTER 5

Growing and Engaging Your Audience

BUILDING A THRIVING COMMUNITY

Let me tell you a little secret about building a thriving community as a content creator. It's not just about putting out awesome content and hoping for the best. No, my friend, it's all about forming meaningful connections with your audience. Picture this: you're sitting down with a cup of coffee, chatting with your best friend about life, dreams, and everything in between. That's the kind of vibe you want to bring to your community.

So, how do you create that personal connection? Well, it starts with showing genuine interest in your followers. Don't just see them as numbers on a screen, but as real people with thoughts, dreams, and unique stories. How do you do that? Engage with them! Respond to their comments, slide into their DMs, and even host live Q&A sessions. Trust me, when you take the time to listen and address their concerns, it builds a bond of trust and authenticity.

But connecting with individuals is just the beginning. You want to create a sense of belonging within your community as a whole. This means giving your followers the chance to connect with each other too. You can set up meetups, organize online events, or create a dedicated Facebook group or forum. The magic happens when friendships blossom and collaborations ignite. Suddenly, your community becomes a hub of inspiration and support.

Now, let's talk about the elephant in the room: moderation. It's necessary for any community to stay healthy and respectful. As a content creator, it's your responsibility to set guidelines and enforce them consistently. Think of it as establishing a code of conduct that outlines the rules of the game. But moderation isn't just about slapping people on the wrist. It's about creating a safe space where everyone feels comfortable expressing their opinions. Healthy debates and discussions? Heck yeah! Toxicity and hate speech? Absolutely not. Keep an eye on the conversations, step in when necessary, and maintain that positive atmosphere.

Here's a thought: why not involve your community in decision-making? Seek their input on future content, ask for ideas on collaborations, or ways to improve the community. When people feel valued, they'll feel a sense of ownership and loyalty. It's like creating a beautiful tapestry together, where everyone's voice matters.

Now, let's talk about creating a sense of belonging within your community. It's all about rituals, traditions, and shared experiences. Treat your community like an exclusive club that throws unforgettable events. Give personalized shoutouts, celebrate milestones, and achievements like virtual parties. When members can identify with these experiences, they'll feel like they're part of something bigger.

But wait, there's more! Don't forget to acknowledge and celebrate the achievements and contributions of your members. Give them the recognition they deserve, whether it's through features on your platforms or sharing their success stories. Provide opportunities for them to shine and showcase their work or talents. By doing so, you empower them and inspire others within the community.

And here's a little secret ingredient: storytelling. Share your own personal experiences, challenges, and triumphs. Let your audience dive deep into your world. But it's not just about you-- encourage your community members to share their stories too. It's like weaving a collective narrative that strengthens the bond between everyone.

So, my friend, building a thriving community as a content creator is an art. It's about fostering meaningful connections, moderating discussions with care, and creating a sense of belonging. When you do that, you'll lay the foundation for a strong and engaged community that will support you and each other on this crazy journey of content creation.

HARNESSING THE POWER OF AUDIENCE INTERACTION

As a content creator, let me tell you, your audience is gold. They're the ones who can take your content to the next level. And in this chapter, we're diving into all the juicy techniques to get them engaged and involved. We're talking Q&A sessions, polls, live chats, and incorporating viewer feedback.

Let's start with Q&A sessions. Picture this: you're going live and your audience is firing questions at you in real-time. It's like having a conversation with them right there. This isn't just about answering questions, it's about making your audience feel heard, making that connection, you know? That's where the magic happens.

Now, when you're hosting a Q&A session, you want to make everyone feel welcome. Lay down the ground rules, like using hashtags or tagging you to ask questions. And let them know exactly when this Q&A extravaganza is going down. It's all about building the hype and getting them excited to participate.

Next up, we've got polls. Imagine giving your audience the power to decide. You're like a content genie, granting their wishes. So, let's say you're a beauty influencer. You could create polls, asking them which products they want you to review or what topics they want you to tackle in your next videos. Give them a chance to voice their opinions and make them feel like rockstars.

Polls can happen anywhere - Instagram, Twitter, YouTube comments - the world is your oyster. And here's a sneaky little tip to boost participation: offer incentives to a lucky poll participant. You could throw in some exclusive sneak peeks or even discount codes. Trust me, they'll be all over it.

Now, let's get real with live chats. This is the

ultimate interactive experience. You're right there, in the moment, hearing their feedback, answering questions, and seeing their reactions. It's like magic. You can host live chats on platforms like YouTube Live, Instagram Live, or Facebook Live.

Pick your poison and dive right in.

But here's the catch - you gotta keep things under control. Set some ground rules, make sure everyone is playing nice, and let the good vibes flow. This way, your audience feels safe and comfortable to ask questions and have meaningful discussions. It's all about creating that sense of community.

Lastly, we can't forget about viewer feedback. Your audience knows what's up. They're your best critics and your biggest fans. So, actively seek out their feedback and incorporate it into your content. This shows them that you value their opinions and that you're dedicated to giving them the best of the best.

There are so many ways to make viewer feedback a part of your content. You can dedicate a segment in your videos or blog posts to address specific comments or suggestions. Take the time to clarify, engage, and show them that you're listening. And hey, don't forget to use analytics and surveys. They give you hard data on what your audience wants. It's like having your own secret weapon to tailor your content to their needs.

To sum it all up, audience interaction is the bread and butter for any content creator. Embrace it and watch your content soar. Use Q&A sessions, polls, live chats, and viewer feedback to empower your audience, add that extra spark, and build a loyal community. Trust me, it's worth every bit of effort.

LEVERAGING SOCIAL MEDIA FOR GROWTH

As I dive into the world of social media, there's one thing I've realized - each platform is like a different universe with its own set of quirks and inhabitants. Facebook, Instagram, Twitter, LinkedIn - they all have their own unique features and demographics that I need to understand if I want my content to make an impact. It's like learning to speak different languages and adapting my style to fit the preferences of each platform's users.

Take Facebook and Instagram, for example. They're all about showing off visually stunning content that makes people stop mid-scroll. It's all about grabbing attention with beautiful images, captivating videos, and catchy captions. But Twitter, oh boy, that's a whole different story. With its annoying character limit, I have to be concise and engaging, like walking a tightrope and making every word count. And let's not forget LinkedIn, the place to be for all things professional and industry-specific. It's like attending a networking event where I have to schmooze and schmooze some more.

But one thing's for sure - visuals are the key to capturing the attention of social media users. People don't have time for boring text-only posts. They want eye candy, they want videos that make their jaws drop, they want content that they can't help but share with their friends. So, I have to put in the effort to create visually stunning content that resonates with my target audience. Luckily, tools like Canva and Adobe Spark make it easier for me to create eye-catching graphics and videos, even if I don't have the skills of a professional designer.

And let me tell you, if there's one thing that's constant in the social media world, it's change. Platforms like Instagram and TikTok are always coming up with new features like Reels and Instagram Guides. It's like they're keeping us on our toes, forcing us to stay relevant and experiment with innovative ways to engage our audience. So, I have to stay on top of the latest trends and embrace these new features to expand my reach and increase my brand visibility.

But it's not just about riding the wave of trends, it's also about analyzing the performance of my content. Thank goodness for built-in analytics tools or third-party platforms that help me understand my audience's behaviors and preferences. Armed with this data, I can make data-driven decisions and optimize my content strategy. If the analytics tell me that my audience is most active on

Instagram in the evenings, then you bet I'll schedule my posts accordingly to get maximum visibility and interaction.

But here's a secret - collaboration is the secret sauce to growth on social media. By teaming up with other content creators or influencers in my niche, I can tap into their audience and gain exposure to a whole new bunch of people. Think about it - featuring each other's content, co-creating amazing stuff, or even organizing joint live sessions or giveaways. It's a win-win situation where I get to boost my visibility and tap into fresh perspectives to create jaw-dropping content for my own audience.

Oh, and let me not forget about engagement. Social media is all about building a community and fostering connections, so I can't just sit back and watch my followers pass by. I have to actively engage with them, respond to their comments, ask them questions, and initiate conversations. It's like building a friendship - just like I can't expect a friend to stick around if I never talk to them, I can't expect my audience to stick around if I don't engage with them. Plus, engaging with influencers and thought leaders in my industry helps me build credibility and expand my network, opening doors to exciting opportunities and collaborations.

But here's the thing - it's all about striking a balance. I need to find the sweet spot between quantity and quality when it comes to my social media presence. Sure, consistency is important and I need to maintain an active presence. But bombarding my audience with mediocre content is a big no-no. Instead, I need to focus on delivering high-quality, value-driven content that truly resonates with my audience. By sharing insights, tips, and solutions to their problems, I can position myself as an authority in my niche and foster a loyal following.

Lastly, and most importantly, I have to be authentic. In a world flooded with content, people crave genuine connections and real stories. So, by showing my true personality, sharing personal experiences, and giving my audience a sneak peek into my behind-the-scenes journey, I can build trust and cultivate a loyal community around my brand. Being authentic not only sets me apart from the countless other content creators out there but also forms the foundation of a lasting and meaningful relationship with my audience.

In conclusion, mastering social media as a content creator is like embarking on a wild adventure. It requires a multi-faceted approach, from tailoring content to platform preferences to embracing emerging trends and analyzing performance. It's a never-ending journey of refining strategies, collaborating with others, and fostering engagement and authenticity. But with each step I take, I can expand my reach, increase brand visibility, and unlock the secrets of the social media universe.

THE ART OF COLLABORATION

Hey there! So, in this digital world of content creation, collaborating with other creators has become a total game-changer. I mean, we're all looking for ways to expand our audience and get those creative juices flowing, right? Well, collaborating gives us the chance to do just that. But, let me tell you, it's not all rainbows and butterflies. There are definitely some challenges we have to tackle along the way. But fear not! In this chapter, I'm going to dive into the nitty-gritty of collaboration, laying out both the benefits and challenges we can expect. Drawing from personal experiences and some solid research, I'll dish out some insights and tips for rocking those collaborations and building relationships that last.

Let's start with the good stuff - the benefits of collaboration. First off, it's like an instant creativity booster shot. When we team up with other creators, we get this incredible mix of ideas and perspectives. It's like a breath of fresh air for our creative process. Our unique talents and expertise come together to create content that resonates with a much larger audience. I'm talking unexpected breakthroughs, innovative concepts, and creations that make people go "wow."

And guess what? Collaboration isn't just good for creativity, it's also a massive audience expander. When we partner up with other creators, we tap into their dedicated fanbase. Suddenly, our content is reaching a whole new audience that might have never found it otherwise. It's a visibility boost, bringing in more traffic and growing our own follower base.

But wait, there's more! Collaboration isn't just about boosting our creativity and reaching more eyes - it's about building genuine relationships too. When we work together and support each other's visions, something magical happens. Trust and loyalty form the foundation of these relationships. And let me tell you, these connections can go way beyond a single collaboration. They can turn into long-term alliances and partnerships that benefit everyone involved.

Of course, it wouldn't be the real world if there weren't some challenges. One big hurdle we face is aligning our creative visions. Every content creator has their own unique style, and when we collaborate, it's not always a perfect match. We might have different preferences, storytelling styles, or even brand values. So, finding that sweet spot between individual creativity and a unified vision takes some serious communication and compromise. The key is to address these challenges early on and find common ground, so the collaboration is a success.

Another challenge is maintaining consistency and quality. When we join forces with other creators, it can be tricky to make sure our content meets both of our high standards. We want to create something that represents both of our styles and keeps our audiences happy. This means we have to collaborate effectively, set clear guidelines, and communicate regularly. When we do it right, the final product is a seamless blend of both our awesomeness.

Time management and coordination also play a big role in collaborations. Let's be real, planning and organizing can be a real pain, especially when we're working with creators from different time zones or with jam-packed schedules. But hey, we've got this. It just takes excellent organization, killer communication, and a commitment to meeting those deadlines.

Okay, now let's get to the good stuff - tips for successful collaborations. First things first, we have to establish clear goals and expectations. Before we start working together, we need to make sure we're all on the same page. That means defining the purpose, scope, and desired outcome of the collaboration. This helps us avoid misunderstandings and conflicts later down the road.

Next up, effective communication is our secret weapon. We need to keep those lines of communication wide open. Whether it's video calls, project management tools, or messaging apps, we've got to stay connected. Regular updates, feedback, and insights are essential for a smooth collaboration. We want to create an environment where problem-solving becomes second nature - a place where everyone feels supported.

Dividing responsibilities and leveraging each other's strengths is also key. We need to play to our strengths and acknowledge that everyone brings something amazing to the table. By doing this, we create a collaboration that showcases the best of both us creators. Divide and conquer, my friends.

Last but not least, we have to embrace flexibility

and adaptability. Collaborations are all about being open to new ideas and alternative approaches. If we're not willing to roll with the punches, we'll miss out on some seriously creative problem-solving and innovation. So, let's be ready to change things up and take feedback like the pros we are.

Okay, one more thing - building those mutually beneficial relationships. Collaborations aren't just about one project. They're about the potential for future partnerships, cross-promotion, and all kinds of exciting ventures. So, let's invest time and effort into nurturing those connections. When we support each other's creative endeavors, share resources and expertise, we become a network of kick-ass content creators that lift each other up. It's all about growing together.

In conclusion, collaboration in content creation is a total powerhouse. It opens up a world of possibilities, expands our reach, and boosts our creativity. But yeah, it's not all smooth sailing. We have to tackle some challenges along the way. Lucky for us, though, with effective communication, compromise, and adaptability, we can totally own collaborations and build relationships that last. Together, we're going to change the game and create unforgettable experiences for our audiences. So, let's do this thing!

NURTURING AUDIENCE LOYALTY

As a content creator, there's nothing like the feeling of knowing my audience is truly engaged and devoted to my work. It's not just about gaining more viewers or followers; it's about building a community that feels like one big family. In this chapter, we're going to dive into the techniques I've discovered to foster long-term audience loyalty. Get ready because this is going to be quite a ride.

Let's start with personalized interactions. One of the most powerful ways to nurture loyalty among your audience is by making them feel seen and heard. As content creators, we have this incredible ability to connect with our viewers on a personal level, and it's crucial to tap into that connection. I've learned that taking the time to respond to comments, messages, and emails goes a long way in building relationships with my audience. When someone takes the time to engage with my content, it's only fair that I reciprocate by showing genuine interest in their thoughts and opinions. This kind of personalized interaction creates a sense of trust and loyalty that's truly invaluable.

In addition, I always try to incorporate my audience's suggestions and ideas into my content whenever possible. By listening and responding to their feedback, I can create content that resonates with them on a deeper level. And here's a little secret - I make an effort to address my audience by their first names, whether it's in written responses or video shout-outs. It's a small gesture, but it makes them feel seen and valued as individuals, rather than just a number in my follower count.

Now, let's talk about exclusive content. This has been a game-changer for me when it comes to nurturing audience loyalty. By offering something exclusive to my most loyal supporters, like bonus videos, behind-the-scenes footage, or even early access to upcoming projects, I show them just how much I appreciate their continued support. This additional value not only keeps them engaged but also encourages them to stick around for more.

But here's the twist - offering exclusive content also acts as a magnet for new members to join my community. When potential followers see that there's more to gain by joining my inner circle, they're motivated to take the leap and become a part of something special. It creates a sense of belonging and fosters a deeper connection between me and my audience.

Next up, rewards programs. Oh, how instrumental they've been in cultivating audience loyalty. By implementing a system where viewers can earn points or rewards for their engagement and support, I incentivize their ongoing participation. This could be as simple as commenting, sharing, or even referring new members to the community. The rewards themselves can vary, from merchandise to personalized shout-outs or even one-on-one video chats.

The secret sauce to a successful rewards program lies in making sure those rewards have meaning and align with the interests and desires of your audience. Once you understand what motivates them, tailoring the rewards accordingly creates a system that truly resonates with your community. This sense of appreciation and recognition strengthens the bond between you and your audience, going beyond just consuming your content.

Last but not least, let's talk about fostering a sense of community ownership. This is absolutely essential when it comes to nurturing audience loyalty. When your audience feels like they have a say in your content and its direction, they become more invested in its success. I've found that actively involving my audience in decision-making processes, such as choosing video topics or even creating content together, not only strengthens our bond but also creates a sense of pride and ownership within the community.

On top of that, creating spaces for community interaction is key. Whether it's through forums, social media groups, or dedicated Discord channels, these platforms allow your audience to connect with each other. The sense of belonging and camaraderie that emerges further reinforces the loyalty they feel towards your content. And here's a little tip - organizing community events, like virtual meetups or live Q&A sessions, provides an opportunity for face-to-face interaction and strengthens the relationships within the community.

To wrap it all up, nurturing audience loyalty is an ongoing process that demands effort, dedication, and a genuine passion for your audience. By implementing personalized interactions, offering exclusive content, establishing rewards programs, and fostering a sense of community ownership, content creators can create an environment where their audience feels valued, engaged, and loyal. Remember, building a loyal, supportive community isn't just about numbers or metrics; it's about creating a family of like-minded individuals who share a common passion. So, go out there and cultivate the loyalty you desire - your audience will be forever grateful for it.

CHAPTER 6

Monetization and Financial Success

DIVERSIFYING REVENUE STREAMS

You know, sponsored content has really become a game-changer for us content creators. It's like this sweet collaboration with brands where we get to promote their stuff and make some serious dough at the same time. We're talking product reviews, sponsored videos, even social media posts that pay the bills. But here's the kicker, we only partner with brands that truly align with our audience and our values. It's not just about the money, it's about building trust and street cred with our viewers, you feel me?

Now, let's talk about another money-making avenue – affiliate marketing. We become affiliates for products or services that we genuinely believe in and actually use ourselves. And here's the kicker again – we earn a commission for every sale made through our special affiliate links. It's like a passive income dream come true. Plus, we get to provide real value to our audience by recommending products that we truly endorse. It's a win-win, baby.

But wait, there's more. We can also launch our own merchandise line and make some bank off our own brand. Picture this: t-shirts, mugs, maybe even some digital goodies like stickers and wallpapers. It's not just about the cash, though. Creating our own merchandise lets us connect with our fans on a whole 'nother level. It gives them a way to support us and show their loyalty in a tangible way. It's like wearing your favorite band's shirt, but better, because it's our stuff.

Now, brace yourself for some suspense. Crowd-funding. Yeah, it's blowing up right now. Platforms like Patreon and Kickstarter are giving us content creators a chance to fund our projects straight from our audience. How, you ask? Well, it's all about offering exclusive perks, early access, and bonus content to our supporters in exchange for their financial love. We can build a community of die-hard fans who are down to support us, so we're not just relying on those pesky ads.

But hold on to your hats, because this is where things get really exciting. We can create digital products, my friend. Picture this: e-books, online courses, presets, templates – you name it! We've got expertise in our niche, and we can package that up into something valuable that our audience is willing to pay for. It's not just about the cash flow (although that's pretty sweet too). It's about establishing ourselves as authorities in our field. It's like leveling up in the content creator game, and getting paid for it.

So, let's talk next steps. First things first, we gotta know our audience inside and out. What do they need? What are their struggles? By doing some market research and engaging with them, we can create content and products that really hit the mark. And then, we gotta build our brand. High-quality content, engaging with our audience, and having a unique voice – that's all part of the game.

Once we've got all that down, it's time to start seeking out sponsorship opportunities. Connect with brands that fit our content and our audience and pitch some killer ideas. Or, hop on platforms like Famebit or Grapevine and let them do the matching for us. Just remember to be transparent with our audience and make sure the products or services we're promoting jive with our values.

And hey, don't forget about affiliate programs. We're gonna need to do some research and find ones that align with our niche and our audience. Look into their reputation, commission rates, and cookie durations. It's all about building trust and maximizing our earnings potential, my friend.

Now, let's get creative with our merchandise. Think about what our audience really digs and design products that speak to them. T-shirts, mugs, you name it. And if we're going digital, make sure those presets and templates are useful, easy to use, and deliver some serious value. Don't be afraid to collaborate with designers or use print-on-demand services to bring our merch ideas to life.

Oh, and crowdfunding. It's time to do some platform research and find the one that's right for us. Craft compelling campaign pitches, show off our value, and really emphasize those exclusive perks for our backers. And you know what? Engage with our audience throughout the whole campaign. Get them excited and build that trust. We're gonna need it to get that sweet, sweet financial support.

And finally, let's get to work on those digital products. We gotta consider our audience's needs and our own expertise. E-books, online courses, presets — whatever floats your boat. But it's gotta be something that solves a problem or delivers some serious value. So, do the research, leverage that expertise, and get those digital products out into the world.

Diversifying our revenue streams? It's not just about the money. It's about expanding our creativity, connecting with our audience, and securing our future. So, let's embrace this opportunity and start getting that cash flow diversified, my friend.

NEGOTIATING BRAND PARTNERSHIPS

So, picture this: you're venturing into the ever-changing world of content creation, exploring uncharted territories, just trying to find that perfect brand collaboration that matches your vibe and values. It's like sailing through uncharted waters, my friend. And let me tell you, the potential to forge meaningful connections and make some serious cash from your creative endeavors is mind-blowing, but it's not a smooth ride. It takes careful consideration, strategic maneuvering, and a killer pitch to stand out in this sea of content creators vying for attention.

Crafting the perfect pitch is like an art form in

itself. You've got to tailor it to reflect the brand's unique identity and objectives, make it scream "this is exactly what you've been looking for!" To do that, start with some serious research. Dive deep into the brand's mission, target audience, and past marketing campaigns. Show them you mean business by demonstrating your knowledge. And then, my friend, let your true strengths shine.

Whether it's your storytelling prowess, your creative vision, or your massive reach, let them know what sets you apart from the rest. But don't stop there - go the extra mile and include specific ideas that align with the brand's objectives. Show them you're committed to making this collaboration a smashing success.

Once you've got their attention, it's time for the negotiation dance. This is where finesse comes into play. You need to know your worth, my friend. Take a deep breath and be clear about your expectations. Talk about deliverables, timelines, exclusivity rights, and of course, compensation. Lay it all out on the table. Let them know what you'll bring to the partnership, whether it's a series of sponsored posts or integrating the brand into a larger campaign. And when it comes to money matters, be informed. Do your research on fair market rates and factor in all the effort and energy you put into creating your content. Advocate for yourself, but also be willing to find a middle ground that both parties can agree on.

Now, let's talk about setting fair rates. I won't lie, it's a challenge. But with a strategic approach, you can do it. Look into industry standards and check out what other creators in your niche are charging. Compare it with your own metrics to get a realistic understanding of your value. And don't forget to consider all the blood, sweat, and tears you pour into creating top-notch content. There are costs involved - planning, shooting, editing, promoting - it all adds up. Your rates should reflect not just the value you bring, but also your need to sustain your creative business in the long run.

But here's the thing, my friend. It's not all about one-time collaborations. Building long-term relationships with brands is the secret sauce to success. It's about cultivating trust, loyalty, and consistent communication. Once you've locked in that partnership, keep those lines of communication open. Check in regularly, professionally, and be responsive to their needs. And when it comes to delivering content, go above and beyond. Exceed expectations. Show them why you're the superstar creator they chose to work with. Trust me, it's all about leaving a lasting impression.

So, to sum it all up, navigating the world of brand partnerships is like sailing through a wild, ever-changing sea. But with killer pitching techniques, smooth negotiations, fair rates, and rock-solid relationships, you can unlock the doors to collaboration and monetization. So go out there, my friend, and thrive in your creative pursuits. The world is yours for the taking.

THE ART OF EFFECTIVE SELF-PROMOTION

Let me start by saying, self-promotion is an absolute must if you want to get your voice out there and be recognized. You've poured your heart and soul into your work, and now it's time to let the world know about it. But listen up, how you promote yourself is what sets you apart. Instead of overwhelming your audience with non-stop self-promotion, it's crucial to focus on making genuine connections and providing value.

So, here's a trick that works like magic: create killer trailers and teasers. These short videos capture the very essence of your content and leave viewers craving for more. When crafting these sneak-peeks, keep it snappy and engaging. Give glimpses of your work that grab attention and keep them hooked. Use visually striking shots, captivating music, or powerful narration to play with their emotions. The key is to create something that resonates with your specific audience and leaves a lasting impact.

But trailers and teasers are just the beginning. Launching full-blown promotional campaigns can fuel excitement and generate some serious interest in your content. The secret sauce here is to be strategic and plan it out. Start by figuring out who your true audience is and what makes them tick. Which platforms do they live on? What kind of content do they devour? Once you've got that down, craft your campaign to cater directly to them.

Now, let me tell you about a total game-changer: social media. Platforms like Instagram, YouTube, and TikTok can be your best friends when it comes to self-promotion. They give you the chance to connect with your audience directly and showcase your work in a visually stunning and captivating way. Building a strong online presence is key to succeeding at self-promotion. Give your followers a glimpse behind the scenes, interact with them, and create a sense of community around your work. Just remember to strike a balance between promoting yourself and offering real value. Share relevant and insightful content related to your niche. Become the go-to expert in your field and build trust with your audience.

But wait, there's more! Collaborations with other content creators are like gold when it comes to self-promotion. Partner up with folks who share a similar target audience and together, you both can reach a wider pool of fans. Collaborations can take many forms - from creating joint content to hosting each other on your platforms. Choose collaborators who align with your brand and can bring true value to your audience. Team up, create some buzz, and tap into new audiences.

Now, don't underestimate the power of good old word-of-mouth promotion. Encourage your existing fans to share your work with their friends and family. Offer them incentives like exclusive content or fun giveaways to motivate them to spread the word. A recommendation from a trusted friend goes a long way in building trust and credibility for your work.

Last but not least, always be authentically you. Audiences can sniff out fakeness from a mile away, and it's a surefire way to lose their trust. Be transparent about your intentions and focus on adding value to their lives. Share your personal journey, your struggles, and your successes. People connect with stories, and by sharing your own, you can forge deep and meaningful connections with your audience.

Self-promotion is an art that requires finesse and

a deep understanding of your audience. By utilizing strategies like creating captivating trailers and teasers, planning strategic promotional campaigns, building a solid online presence, collaborating with other content creators, encouraging word-of-mouth promotion, and staying true to yourself, you can conquer the realm of self-promotion. Just remember, the endgame is to share your passion with the world and make a positive impact. With effective self-promotion, you can achieve just that.

FINANCIAL PLANNING AND MANAGEMENT

Let me tell you, financial planning can be a real maze, especially when you're a content creator. Trust me, I've been there. As someone who works independently, you're basically a self-employed individual, which means you're in charge of paying your own taxes. And let me tell you, the world of self-employment tax laws is no joke. It's like walking through a minefield blindfolded.

That's why it's crucial to consult with a tax

professional who specializes in working with content creators. Believe me, they can help you navigate through all the rules and regulations, and minimize the risk of future financial burdens. You definitely don't want the taxman knocking on your door, demanding a hefty sum because you didn't dot your i's and cross your t's.

But hey, taxes are not the only thing you need to worry about. Managing your finances effectively is a whole other ball game. Luckily, there are some amazing accounting tools out there that can make your life so much easier. I'm talking about QuickBooks and Excel. These tools are like secret weapons for content creators. They simplify financial tracking and reporting, which can be a real headache. With a few clicks, you can organize your income and expenses, generate profit and loss statements, and even get ready for tax season. It's like having a personal financial wizard at your fingertips.

Now, let's talk about budgeting. I know, it sounds boring and restrictive, but trust me, it's essential. Without a budget, it's like sailing on a ship without a compass. You'll end up going in circles and wasting your hard-earned cash. When creating a budget, make sure to consider both fixed and variable expenses. Fixed expenses are the ones that stay pretty much the same month after month, like rent, utilities, and software subscriptions. On the other hand, variable expenses like equipment upgrades, marketing costs, and travel expenses can fluctuate like crazy. So, keep an eye on those and make sure to allocate your income wisely.

Now, let's dive into saving and investing, my favorite part. As content creators, our income can be quite unpredictable. Some months we're swimming in cash, and other months we're scrounging for pennies. That's why it's crucial to have some savings to fall back on when those slow months hit you like a ton of bricks. Trust me, it's a lifesaver. I recommend setting aside a percentage of each paycheck, let's say 10% or even more if you can swing it. This will build up your emergency fund and help you weather any unexpected storms. And if you're feeling really adventurous, consider long-term investments like retirement accounts or real estate. They can provide you with a more secure financial future, even when you're old and gray.

Oh, and let's not forget about diversifying your income streams. You know what they say, don't put all your eggs in one basket. As content creators, we often rely on ad revenue or brand partnerships, which can be great, but what happens if one of those streams dries up? That's why it's smart to explore other opportunities. You can create digital products, take on freelance work, or even start a Patreon page. The sky's the limit, my friend. By diversifying your income, you'll not only minimize the risk of relying too heavily on one source but also increase your overall financial stability. It's a win-win situation.

Now, let's fast forward to the future. Retirement planning. Yeah, I know, it's the last thing on your mind when you're busy creating amazing content. But trust me, neglecting retirement planning can come back to bite you. Hard. So, take a moment to consider individual retirement accounts (IRAs) or simplified employee pension (SEP) IRAs. They can be your lifeline when you're finally ready to hang up your camera. And don't forget to consult with a financial advisor who knows the ins and outs of retirement planning. They'll guide you through the process and help you make the right decisions.

Lastly, let's talk insurance. Yeah, I know, it's not the sexiest topic, but stick with me here. As content creators, we face risks every day. Equipment damage, theft, liability issues, and even health concerns. It's no joke. But fear not, my friend, because there are insurance policies out there that can protect you from unforeseen circumstances. Whether it's equipment insurance, liability insurance, or even disability insurance, investing in coverage tailored to your needs will give you peace of mind and protect your financial well-being. Trust me, it's worth every penny.

So, there you have it. Financial planning and management might seem like a daunting task, but if you follow these strategies, you'll be on your way to long-term financial stability. You'll be able to focus on what you do best – creating amazing content that resonates with your audience. So, buckle up, my friend, and get ready for the incredible journey ahead.

CREATING A SUSTAINABLE BUSINESS MODEL

So, you wanna know how to create a sustainable business as a content creator, huh? Well, let me tell ya, diversification is the name of the game. You can't rely on just one platform or source of income, that's way too risky. Imagine if you're getting all your dough from ad revenue on one social media platform, and then bam! They change their algorithms or policies. Suddenly, your wallet is feelin' a little light, if you catch my drift.

To avoid this kinda nightmare, you gotta diversify your income streams. Get creative, explore new monetization options. Start slappin' some sponsored content on your platform, get into that affiliate marketing gig, or even slap your name on some merchandise. Shoot, you could even launch your own products or services. The key is to have multiple streams of income flowin' in, so if one dries up, you've still got others to rely on. Plus, the more ways you're makin' money, the more green you'll be stackin'.

Now, on to scalability. You don't wanna sacrifice the quality of your content, but you do wanna reach a bigger audience. So, how do you do that without pullin' your hair out? Well, honey, you gotta find ways to scale your business. That means hiring a team to help churn out content, outsourcing tasks that aren't your strong suit, or using automation tools to make your life a little easier. By scaling up, you'll be crankin' out content like nobody's business, and that means more eyes on your stuff and more dough in your pocket.

Partnerships, my friend, can be a real game-changer. Collaboratin' with other creators or brands is like a two-for-one special. You get exposed to new audiences, and you open up new ways to bring in that moolah. Now, when it comes to partners, don't just jump into bed with anyone. You gotta find someone whose values and target audience align with yours. That way, the collab will benefit both of ya and bring in some real results.

Plus, partnerships can lead to cross-promotion opportunities, which means more people findin' out about you and your content. Double win, my friend.

Lastly, you gotta have a plan for long-term growth and stability. Set clear goals, develop a solid content strategy, and always be analyzing and tweakin' your approach. Try new things, experiment with different formats or topics. Keep an eye on trends and what's happenin' in your industry. And don't forget to invest in yourself, keep learnin', and stay ahead of the pack. With all these pieces in place, you'll be the top dog in your niche and have a business that'll stand the test of time.

So there you have it, my friend. Building a sustainable business as a content creator ain't easy, but with some smart planning, hard work, and a dash of creativity, you can turn your passion into a thriving empire. It won't happen overnight, but trust me, it'll be worth it in the end. Now go out there and make your mark in the digital world!

CHAPTER 7

Overcoming Creative Blocks

BREAKING THROUGH MENTAL BARRIERS

You know what's a real pain in the creative pants? Self-doubt. It's like having this annoying voice in my head that just won't shut up. It keeps asking me, "Are you really good enough? Is your work what it should be?" And man, let me tell you, those thoughts can really mess with your mojo. It's like I'm constantly second-guessing myself and it's hard to break free from that mental trap.

But you know what? I'm starting to learn a

thing or two about dealing with this self-doubt monster. First off, I've realized that I gotta show myself some love. I mean, come on, nobody's perfect, right? Instead of focusing on my flaws, I'm learning to celebrate even the tiniest achievements. Every step forward, no matter how small, is a win. And you know what? It's amazing how much that can boost my confidence.

But self-doubt isn't the only barrier I've had to face on this creative journey. There's also this nagging fear of failure that likes to show up uninvited. It's like this dark cloud hanging over my head, telling me that my work won't be appreciated or understood. And let me tell you, that fear can really put a damper on your creativity.

But here's the thing, failure isn't the end of the world. It's like going on a rollercoaster ride – sometimes you go up, and sometimes you come crashing down. But you know what? Those crashes are just part of the journey. They're lessons in disguise, teaching me what works and what doesn't. So now, instead of fearing failure, I embrace it. I see it as an opportunity to grow and learn. And let me tell you, that shift in mindset has opened up a world of possibilities.

Okay, let's talk about perfectionism. You know, that little voice that always wants everything to be flawless? Yeah, that voice can be a real buzzkill. It's like this relentless pursuit of perfection that drains the joy out of creating. But guess what? Creativity isn't meant to be perfect. It's messy, it's imperfect, and that's what makes it beautiful.

So now, I'm learning to let go of my obsession with perfection. I'm realizing that progress is more important than trying to achieve some unattainable ideal. And you know what? It's liberating. I can take risks, explore new ideas, and create content that's authentic to me. And let me tell you, that's when the magic happens.

But you know what? I would be lying if I said I did this all on my own. Having a supportive community of fellow creators has been a game-changer. You meet these amazing people who get it. They understand the struggles, the self-doubt, and the fear of failure. And let me tell you, when you have that kind of support, it makes all the difference. They inspire you, encourage you, and remind you that you're not alone in this crazy creative journey.

Look, breaking through these mental barriers is an ongoing battle. They're always going to be there, lurking in the shadows. But you know what? I refuse to let them hold me back. I'm going to use them as fuel for growth and keep pushing forward. Because that's what being a content creator is all about – conquering those doubts, fears, and perfectionist tendencies. So, let's go on this wild ride together, and uncover the untold secrets of content creators. It's not going to be easy, but man, it's going to be worth it.

CULTIVATING A CREATIVE MINDSET

Alright, folks, let me tell you about this game-changer called mindfulness. It's been an absolute game-changer for me in my creative journey. Seriously, it's like magic. Mindfulness is all about being in the here and now, fully aware of your thoughts and actions. It's like hitting the mute button on all the noise in your mind so you can focus on what's really important.

When I get into that mindful state, it's like I'm in another dimension. I can actually observe my thoughts and ideas without any judgment holding me back. It's a space where my creativity can run wild. It's like setting your mind free in a vast open field. Trust me, it's liberating.

Now, to get into this awesome mindset, I start my day with a little meditation. Picture this: I find a quiet spot, close my eyes, and just let go. I bring my attention to my breath, inhaling and exhaling, and truly feeling every little sensation. I let go of all those pesky thoughts and distractions. It's just me and my breath, baby.

Let me tell you, this simple act of mindfulness sets the stage for a kick-ass day. It's like my mind becomes this clear, peaceful lake, and it stays that way throughout the day. Mental clarity, my friends, that's what it's all about.

But it's not just mindfulness that gets my creative juices flowing. Oh no, there's more. You see, I'm all about pushing the boundaries and trying new things. That's how we grow as creators, right? So I embrace experimentation like it's my own personal challenge.

I dabble in all sorts of mediums and formats. I'm talking video editing, writing styles you've never even heard of, and jumping into the world of graphic design. It's like a rollercoaster ride for my creativity. And let me tell you, each new adventure lights a fire under my ass. It makes me think outside the box and keeps my mind fresh and pumped with new ideas.

Oh, and let's not forget about that growth-oriented perspective. This mindset is crucial if you wanna be a kick-ass creator. You see, it's all about believing that you can develop your skills and abilities through hard work and dedication. No limits, baby.

So when I'm faced with failure or challenges, guess what? I don't sweat it. I see it as an opportunity for growth. It's like these setbacks are stepping stones to greatness. I approach every project with curiosity and resilience, knowing that even if it doesn't turn out like I expected, I can always improve and grow.

Now, I didn't just stumble upon these practices overnight. I did my research, my friend. I wanted to know what the successful content creators were doing. And let me tell you, they got some rituals, man. You wouldn't believe what a little structure and consistency can do for your creativity.

One thing these creators do is carve out dedicated time for their craft. They set aside specific hours or even whole days where they shut out the world and dive deep into their creative process. It's intentional, it's focused, and it's where the magic happens.

But that's not all. They're all about seeking inspiration from diverse sources. They're like sponges, soaking up new experiences, different art forms, and immersing themselves in all sorts of cultures and perspectives. They're like the ultimate adventurers, always on the lookout for fresh ideas that can fuel their creativity. It keeps things exciting and adds a unique twist to their content.

Look, I've learned a lot on this creative journey of mine. Cultivating a creative mindset is no cakewalk. It takes dedication, discipline, and a whole lotta growth mindset. But let me tell you, it's worth it. So worth it.

I know it's a solitary road, but with this creative mindset in your toolbox, you can tap into an endless well of inspiration. You can transform your creative process into something fulfilling and enriching. It's like unlocking a secret power within yourself.

So hey, join me on this wild ride. Let's explore together as we uncover the untold secrets of content creators. We'll dive into resilience, the art of storytelling, and the importance of self-care. All crucial stuff on our journey to becoming kick-ass content creators.

With every turn of the page, my hope is to

spark something within you. To ignite a fire that says, "Damn it, I'm creative and I'm ready to share my voice with the world." Because trust me, my friend, the untold secrets of content creators are waiting to be unleashed. And I'm honored to be your guide on this mind-blowing journey.

FINDING INSPIRATION IN UNLIKELY PLACES

So, here's the deal: as a content creator, I've learned that inspiration can be found in the most unexpected places. Sure, it's important to stay in the loop and keep up with the trends, but let me tell you, tapping into those unlikely sources has breathed new life into my work.

Nature, my friend. Yeah, it's like this limitless pool of inspiration right outside our doors. The beauty of the natural world is downright awe-inspiring. It can ignite a sense of wonder and spark ideas like nothing else. Whether it's the vibrant colors of a breathtaking sunset, the chorus of birds chirping at the crack of dawn, or the tranquil stillness of a forest, nature has a way of connecting us to our creative selves. Personally, I find solace in long walks through the woods or sitting by a peaceful lakeside. It's like disconnecting from the digital circus and tapping into a deep well of inspiration. The intricate patterns on a leaf or the delicate petals of a flower, man, they can trigger new ideas and give my content creation a fresh perspective.

Now, let's talk art. Don't sleep on the art world, my friend. Hitting up art galleries or museums can give you a dose of creative juice that'll make your head spin. Art offers a whole buffet of inspiration. I, for one, am always drawn to those vibrant colors in impressionist paintings or the bold and out-of-the-box lines of abstract art. By diving into an artist's expression, I can find new ways to communicate my message and capture my audience's attention. Adding elements of art to my work, like playing with color schemes or putting together visually stunning visuals, gives my content that unique and captivating touch.

And then there's travel, my favorite escape route. Not only does it broaden your horizons, but it's also like a treasure map to inspiration. Stepping out of your comfort zone and immersing yourself in new cultures and landscapes? Man, it's a gold mine for fresh ideas. Whether you're getting lost in the hustle and bustle of a city or basking in the tranquility of a remote village, every new destination gives you a chance to see the world from a different angle. When I'm surrounded by unfamiliar sights, sounds, and flavors, I uncover fresh perspectives and narratives that I incorporate into my content. It could be a dope travelogue, a deep dive into a culture, or just infusing elements of a foreign land into my work. Travel has become my secret weapon for inspiration.

Now, I know we can't forget about literature. Books, my friend, they're like a direct line to inspiration. Don't underestimate the power of the written word. Classics, poetry, thought-provoking non-fiction – they're packed with ideas, emotions, and intellectual stimulation. Reading lets us dive into whole new worlds, encounter fascinating characters, and explore complex themes. When I crack open a book, I find the vivid descriptions and mind-blowing insights can really inspire me to create content that hits deep in the hearts of my audience. Drawing upon the themes, imagery, and storytelling techniques from literature, I can craft content that transports my readers to another realm.

But here's the thing: it's not just about finding inspiration in unconventional places. It's all about how you integrate those influences into your work. Here are a few tricks I've picked up along the way:

First, abstract associations. Instead of straight-up copying what inspired you, try to abstract or reinterpret the essence of it. This way, you create something fresh and original while still capturing that unconventional inspiration.

Next up, the synthesis of ideas. Combine inspiration from different sources in innovative ways. Mix and match seemingly unrelated concepts to create a unique blend that adds depth and intrigue to your content.

Then there's metaphorical storytelling. Use metaphors and symbolism to infuse your content with the essence of those unconventional inspirations.

Borrow storytelling techniques from literature and connect with your audience on a deeper level.

And finally, my friend, don't be afraid to experiment. Step out of that comfort zone. Incorporate those unconventional sources of inspiration into your creative process and try different formats, styles, and techniques. Keep your work fresh and exciting.

So, listen up, my fellow creators. Approach the world with an open mind and a curious spirit, because inspiration is lurking in every corner. Go explore the unconventional, and who knows, you might just stumble upon your most remarkable and captivating ideas yet.

TECHNIQUES FOR IDEA GENERATION

You know, one of the toughest things we, as content creators, have to deal with is constantly coming up with new and exciting ideas. It's like the demand for fresh content never stops, and it can be downright overwhelming. But fear not! I'm here to save the day. In this chapter, I'm gonna let you in on some practical techniques to generate ideas that will ensure you never run out of inspiration again.

Now, let's kick things off with brainstorming exercises. It's probably one of the most tried-and-true methods to get those creative juices flowing. Picture this: you're in a room with a diverse group of folks, each with their own unique perspectives and experiences. It's like a creative melting pot. The key is to create an environment that encourages everyone to share their ideas without fear of judgment or criticism. Trust me, that's when the magic happens.

During a brainstorming session, let your imagination run wild. Think outside the box, challenge the status quo, and explore uncharted territories. Heck, throw out some outrageous ideas while you're at it. You'd be surprised how often those wild notions lead to something truly innovative. And don't worry about the practicality or feasibility of your ideas at this stage. The goal is to get as many ideas on the table as possible.

Now, let's move on to mind mapping. This technique is all about visually organizing your thoughts and concepts in a way that's not all linear and boring. Imagine a giant sheet of paper or a mind mapping software. Start off by writing your central idea in the middle and then branch out from there, jotting down related ideas and keywords. Connect the dots, find patterns, and discover unexpected connections. It's like your thoughts are weaving this intricate web of creativity.

I love mind mapping because it gives you a visual representation of your thought process. You can see your ideas laid out in front of you, making it easier to spot gaps, overlaps, and areas that need a bit more exploring. Plus, mind mapping lets your mind wander freely, increasing the chances of stumbling upon those unconventional, out-of-the-box ideas. It's like exploring the uncharted territory of your own imagination.

Next up, we've got free writing. This one's all about breaking through those creative blocks and tapping into your subconscious. Picture yourself in a quiet, cozy space, free from distractions. Give yourself a prompt or a topic to focus on, and then just write. No stopping, no editing, just let your thoughts flow onto the paper or screen. Even if it seems like gibberish at first, keep going. Trust me on this.

Free writing is all about bypassing your inner critic and judgment. It's about creating a safe space for your subconscious mind to reveal its hidden treasures. Once you've finished your writing spree, go back and dig into what you've written. You might be surprised at the gems you uncover. There could be interesting ideas or connections just waiting to be developed further.

Last but not least, let's talk about the power of collaboration. Sometimes, the best ideas are born when minds collide. Working with others can fuel your creativity and lead to breakthroughs you might not have stumbled upon on your own. Imagine combining different perspectives, expertise, and experiences. It's like diving into a vast pool of ideas and insights.

When collaborating, it's essential to create an inclusive and supportive environment. One where open communication and participation are encouraged. Lay out clear goals and expectations, so everyone knows what they're working towards. And hey, don't forget to listen actively and give everyone a chance to contribute their ideas. Collaboration can come in many forms – from structured brainstorming sessions to ongoing partnerships or even casual chats with fellow creators. Just foster an environment where ideas can flow freely and watch the magic happen.

So, my friend, generating fresh and innovative ideas is the name of the game in content creation. And with these techniques – brainstorming exercises, mind mapping, free writing, and collaboration – you'll be igniting your creative fire and unlocking a world of possibilities. Remember, approach idea generation with an open mind and a willingness to dig into the unconventional. Embrace the process, and let your ideas flourish. Soon enough, you'll never find yourself at a loss for inspiration again.

EMBRACING FAILURE AS A CATALYST FOR GROWTH

You know, failure gets a bad rap sometimes. We're taught to avoid it at all costs, like it's this big, scary monster standing between us and success. But what if I told you that failure could actually be a good thing? What if I told you that it could be the key to growth and success? Well, in the world of content creation, failure is not only normal, but it's actually necessary. It's through our failures that we learn, innovate, and ultimately reach our goals. So, in this chapter, we're going to dive deep into the role failure plays in the creative process, look at some famous examples of people who failed their way to success, and discover strategies for embracing failure as a stepping stone to growth.

Let me tell you, the creative process is far from smooth sailing. It's more like a roller coaster ride, filled with twists, turns, and moments that make your stomach drop. As content creators, we're constantly pushing the boundaries, trying new things, and taking risks. But the fear of failure can hold us back from reaching our full potential. We doubt ourselves, we second-guess our ideas, and we let that fear keep us from truly shining.

But you know what? Failure isn't something to be afraid of. Failure is something to be embraced. Just look at Thomas Edison. He once said, "I have not failed. I've just found 10,000 ways that won't work." Can you imagine that? 10,000 failures before finally creating the light bulb! Each failure was a stepping stone, bringing him closer and closer to his ultimate success. Edison understood that failure was just a part of the creative process, and that's what made him one of the greatest inventors of all time.

And then there's J.K. Rowling, the mastermind behind the Harry Potter series. Before becoming a household name, she faced rejection after rejection from publishers. They said her story was too long, too complicated, and that there was no market for it. But did Rowling let that stop her? Nope. She used those setbacks as fuel to improve her writing and keep pursuing her dream. And look at her now – one of the most successful authors in the world, inspiring millions of readers across the globe.

These stories show us the power of embracing failure as a catalyst for growth. Failure doesn't define us or our abilities. It's an opportunity to learn, adapt, and grow. So, here are some strategies to help you embrace failure and use it to your advantage.

First, shift your mindset. Instead of viewing failure as a personal failure, see it as a chance to learn and grow. It's just a natural part of the creative process. When you approach failure with curiosity and resilience, you'll see it in a whole new light.

Next, learn from your failures. Every failure has a lesson to teach. Take the time to reflect on what went wrong, what you could have done differently, and how you can apply those learnings in the future. Failure is your chance to grow and improve as a content creator.

Another strategy is to surround yourself with support. Seek out other creators who have experienced failure and can offer guidance and encouragement. Share your failures with them and learn from each other's experiences. Together, you can grow and overcome any obstacle.

Now, taking risks is a big part of the creative process, and with risks comes the possibility of failure. But not all risks are created equal. So, take calculated risks. Evaluate the potential risks and rewards before diving headfirst into a new project or idea. This way, you can minimize the negative outcomes and maximize the potential for growth and success.

Lastly, celebrate your small victories. In the face of failure, it's easy to forget about the small wins along the way. But those wins are signs of progress and growth. They show you how far you've come and remind you of your resilience and determination. Embracing failure isn't a one-time thing – it's an ongoing journey.

So, my friend, failure is just a part of the creative process. It's not something to be afraid of. Without failure, there can be no growth. Embracing failure as a catalyst for growth allows us to approach our work fearlessly and with resilience.

By reframing failure as a learning opportunity, we can learn from our mistakes, adapt, and ultimately achieve success. So, don't let the fear of failure hold you back. Embrace it, learn from it, and let it propel you towards your creative aspirations.

CHAPTER 8

Navigating Legal and Copyright Issues

UNDERSTANDING FAIR USE AND COPYRIGHT

As a content creator, let me tell you something. Understanding fair use and copyright is no joke. It's like stepping into a minefield, with debates and questions ready to explode all around you. You end up wondering what is actually allowed and what will land you in legal trouble when using copyrighted material. So, in this chapter, we're gonna dive deep into the crazy concept of fair use, how it applies to content creation, and all the legal mumbo jumbo you need to keep in mind.

But before we get into the nitty-gritty, let me throw a thought at you. What the heck is fair use? Simple answer - it's a legal cloak that lets us use copyrighted stuff without begging permission from the copyright owner. It's like a magic wand that makes our content creation journey possible. We can riff off existing works, twist them, turn them, and create something wonderfully new.

But hold up! Fair use isn't this one-size-fits-all kind of deal. Nope, it's got rules, limitations, and all that jazz. We gotta keep our heads screwed on tight and understand that fair use isn't a free-for-all pass to use copyrighted material however we want. It's more like a tightrope act, balancing our creative interests with the rights of those copyright holders.

So, to make sure we're on the right side of the law, we need to consider four key factors. They are like our superhero squad, coming to the rescue whenever fair use questions arise. We got the purpose and character of the use, the nature of the copyrighted work, the amount and substantiality of what we use, and the impact on the market for the original work.

Let's break it down, shall we? Purpose and character of the use is all about how we use that copyrighted stuff. Courts dig it when we transform the original work into something fresh and different. You know, like when we take quotes from a novel for a book review and analyze them. That's fair use. But if we just copy someone else's work without adding any of our own flair, well, that's a big no-no in the fair use game.

Now, let's talk about the nature of the copyrighted work. It's like the personality of the original creation. If it's a nonfiction or informational piece, it's more likely to get a fair use green light. That's because the law recognizes the importance of spreading knowledge for the good of society. So, if you're using a factual work, you can breathe a little easier.

But hang on a second! The amount and substantiality of what we use also matter. There's no magic percentage or word count that defines fair use - it's more of an art than a science. But here's the deal: using a small portion of a copyrighted work is usually safer than throwing the entire thing into our own content. And watch out, using the juiciest parts of a work could come back to bite us. If we're taking away the market's appetite for the original, fair use might not be in our cards.

Last but not least, we have the impact on the market for the original work. Yep, money talks. If our use of the copyrighted stuff crushes the market value or potential sales of the original, fair use isn't gonna be our salvation. The law isn't too keen on messing with the economics of creativity, you know?

But here's the thing. These factors aren't always the fair use gospel. Nope, every situation is unique and must be treated that way. It's like solving a mystery, Sherlock Holmes style. You need to examine the specificities and circumstances of each use. And hey, don't forget to consult the wise ones - legal professionals or copyright experts. They'll guide you through the maze and help you dodge infringement claims.

So, here's what it all boils down to, my fellow content creators. Knowing your limits and the legal stuff when it comes to copyrighted material is a big deal. It lets you navigate the tricky world of intellectual property rights with style. And it also encourages your creative juices to flow while playing nice with others. By embracing fair use and applying it wisely, you can take inspiration from existing works, add your own magic touch, and contribute to the grand symphony of content creation in a responsible and ethical fashion.

Now, hold on to your hats, because in the next chapter, we're diving into the enchanting land of monetization. We'll uncover all the secret strategies content creators use to make a buck from their creations. Trust me, it's gonna be one heck of a ride as we unlock the mysterious power of transforming passion into profit. So, join me, my friend, and let's embark on this adventure together.

LICENSING AND PERMISSIONS

Obtaining licenses and permissions may not be the most exciting part of being a content creator, but it's essential for fostering collaboration and respect within our creative community. Think of it as a way of showing love and appreciation for the original creators. Plus, it's not just about legality, it's also about being ethically responsible.

So, where do we begin? One crucial step in this process is identifying the copyrighted material we want to use. Whether it's music tracks, photos, videos, or even written content, we need to know what we're working with. Luckily, there are licensing platforms out there that cater to different types of media. All we have to do is research and find the platforms that suit our needs.

Let's start with music. One popular licensing platform is Soundstripe. They have a vast library of royalty-free music that content creators can use without any restrictions. It's like having a treasure trove of tunes at our disposal. By subscribing to platforms like Soundstripe, we can access a wide range of music tailored to our specific project requirements.

Now, what about images? Creative Commons licenses are a great resource for this. These licenses give us the green light to use images under specific conditions set by the original creators. It's like having a framework of rules that ensures we're playing fair. Websites like Unsplash and Pixabay fall under this category, offering a massive collection of high-quality images that we can use without needing explicit permissions. It's like having an art gallery at our fingertips.

And what about videos? Platforms like Shutterstock and Pond5 have us covered. They offer a comprehensive range of stock footage and clips that we can license and use to enhance our creative projects. It's like having a library of visual goodies waiting for us. Not only do these platforms provide valuable resources for content creators, but they also make sure the original creators get their fair share of recognition and compensation.

Now, let's talk legal stuff. Unauthorized use

of copyrighted material can lead to serious consequences, from legal penalties to damaging our reputation. We don't want that, do we? So, it's crucial to familiarize ourselves with copyright laws and regulations. Trust me, it's worth it. Because when it comes to using copyrighted material without permission, there's something called fair use. It's a concept that allows for limited use of copyrighted material, but it's a bit tricky and subjective. We need to consider four factors: the purpose and character of the use, the nature of the copyrighted work, the amount used, and the effect on the market for the original work. Sounds complicated, but it's necessary to understand if our use falls under fair use or if we need to seek explicit permissions. When in doubt, it's always better to be safe than sorry.

So, how do we go about seeking permissions? Well, it's all about being methodical and professional. First, identify the copyright holder. Do some good ol' research or, better yet, reach out to the creator or their representatives directly. Once you find them, craft a well-written permission request. Keep it concise and formal, but also show your appreciation for their work and assure them that you'll attribute and compensate them properly. The more information you provide about your project, its scope, and the intended audience, the more likely they'll be to grant those permissions.

Sometimes, copyright holders may ask for a licensing fee or specific conditions. It's important to negotiate and reach a fair agreement that satisfies everyone involved. This could include details such as the duration, territories, and limitations of use, as well as determining the appropriate compensation for the copyright holder.

In conclusion, licensing and permissions are like the unsung heroes of the content creation world. They guide us in acquiring the necessary rights for using copyrighted material, help us explore awesome licensing platforms, and keep us on the right side of the law. So, as content creators, let's embrace this process. Through mutual respect and collaboration, our work can truly thrive.

PROTECTING INTELLECTUAL PROPERTY

Alright, gather around my fellow content creators, because in this chapter of "Untold Secrets of Content Creators," I'm about to drop some knowledge bombs on intellectual property protection. Yep, that's right. We're diving into the world of copyright registration, trademarks, and all the strategies we need to employ to keep our creative work safe from those sneaky infringers. Buckle up, it's about to get real.

First things first, copyright registration is like our superhero cape when it comes to protecting our creative work. By getting our work registered with the copyright office, we're basically saying, "Hey, this is mine, and I own all the rights to reproduce, distribute, display, and perform it." It covers everything from our written masterpieces, beautiful art, toe-tapping music, mind-boggling films, to even software wizardry.

So, how do we kickstart this copyright registration process? Well, we gotta file an application with the copyright office. This baby usually asks for details like the title of our work, when we created it, and a nice little description. Oh, and don't forget to include a copy of the work itself to prove its originality. Now, here's the kicker - our work is automatically protected by copyright upon creation, but registering it has some sweet benefits. Not only does it create a public record of our ownership (mic drop), but it also gives us the power to seek legal remedies if someone decides to mess with our precious creation. Money talks, my friends, and in this case, it's all about damages and attorney fees.

Now, hold onto your hats because we're about to slide into the world of trademarks. Trademarks are all about protecting our names, logos, and other symbols that make our brand or products stand out in this crazy competitive market. We've gotta register these bad boys to claim exclusive rights to use and safeguard our brand identity. It's like trying to keep our competitors at bay and keep our reputation intact. No room for confusion, people!

To get trademark protection, we gotta file an application with the trademark office. They'll want all the deets like what our mark looks like, what goods or services it's associated with, and proof that we're using it in commerce. Unlike copyright, trademarks need constant nurturing and enforcement to keep that exclusivity going strong. So, we gotta keep a close eye on the marketplace, sniff out any potential infringement, and rain down fire and brimstone in the form of legal action when needed.

But wait, there's more! Apart from all the legal stuff, we've got a bunch of strategies up our sleeve to guard our precious work. One of them is establishing a strong online presence and being proactive in enforcing our rights via digital platforms. We gotta become the Sherlock Holmes of the online world, folks. By keeping an eye on websites, social media platforms, and online marketplaces, we can spot any unauthorized use of our content and swiftly take it down using the Digital Millennium Copyright Act (DMCA). These online platforms are our trusty sidekicks, ready to lend a hand in reporting infringement and protecting our intellectual property.

Oh, but it doesn't stop there! We can also bring in some ninja-level technology to protect our work. I'm talking about digital rights management techniques, like encryption and watermarking. These superpowers make it harder for thieves to go unnoticed and provide solid evidence for legal battles. Boom!

Now, you know what's even cooler? Licensing agreements. Yep, we can control the use and distribution of our work by granting limited rights to others. We're the bosses, baby! These agreements allow us to lay down the law with terms and conditions, royalty payments, and enforcement mechanisms if someone tries to pull a fast one. Not only do they protect our stuff, but they also provide opportunities for collaboration and more moolah in our pockets. Win-win!

But hold up, my fellow creators. While it's crucial to safeguard our own intellectual property, we also gotta be mindful of others' rights. We can't just go willy-nilly incorporating third-party content into our creations without obtaining the proper permissions, licenses, or making sure it falls under fair use or similar exceptions. We gotta be the change in the creative community, setting an example for ethical content creation.

So, to sum it all up, protecting our intellectual property is the name of the game, my friends. We've gotta wrap our heads around copyright registration, trademarks, and the strategies that keep our work safe. By doing this, we ensure that our blood, sweat, and tears get the recognition and rewards they rightfully deserve. As content creators, we hold the power to take proactive measures in protecting our intellectual property while respecting the rights of others. Together, we'll create a thriving creative ecosystem that celebrates innovation, collaboration, and the preservation of originality. Let's do this!

AVOIDING LEGAL PITFALLS

Let me tell you, being a content creator is no walk in the park. We're constantly walking through a minefield of legal issues like defamation, privacy violations, and libel. One wrong move, and boom! Our reputation goes up in smoke, and we might even find ourselves in a nasty court battle. Trust me, that's the last thing we want.

Defamation is like a ticking time bomb. It's when you go around spreading false information that ruins someone's good name. As content creators, we gotta be careful with our words. We need to make sure we're spitting out the truth and backing it up with solid evidence. Spreading lies can land us in deep trouble, with lawsuits and a shattered reputation as consequences. And nobody wants that, right?

To stay clear of defamation landmines, we gotta do our homework. That means digging deep, fact-checking, and making sure our sources are legit. We can't be lazy about it. And hey, it's essential to distinguish between our opinions and facts. Making it crystal clear that something is just our take on things puts a shield between us and potential defamation claims. Safety first, right?

Now, let's talk privacy violations. Man, oh man,

these are dangerous waters to navigate. In this day and age, where personal info is just a click away, respecting people's privacy is golden. Sharing someone's private stuff without their consent is a recipe for disaster. Not only can we end up in legal hot water, but we'll also lose the trust of our audience. And believe me, that's a tough pill to swallow.

To avoid those privacy landmines, we need to get permission before we spill the beans. It's simple, really. Just ask nicely or use those fancy legal release forms when necessary. And let's not forget about securing our platforms and databases. We don't want anybody hacking into our stuff and spreading everyone's private info, do we? No way!

Oh, and let's not forget about libel. This beast is like defamation's evil twin, but in written form. And with the power of the internet, our words can travel at the speed of light, making libel an even bigger threat. If we start throwing false accusations and damaging statements out there, we better be ready for the legal storm that follows. It ain't pretty, my friend.

To dodge the libel bullets, we gotta prioritize the truth. We have to make sure our statements are backed up by reliable sources, and it wouldn't hurt to present a balanced view of things too. Fact-checking and seeking legal guidance on sensitive topics can be our secret weapon in this game.

And trust me, it's a game we don't wanna lose.

Alright, enough talk about the landmines. Let's focus on how to avoid them altogether. We need some solid strategies to minimize those legal risks, my friend. First things first – reviewing and keeping up with the ever-changing laws. Yeah, I know, it sounds like a drag, but it's a necessary evil. Knowledge is power, after all.

And copyright? Oh boy, don't get me started. We need to make sure we're not stepping on anyone's creative toes. Familiarizing ourselves with copyright laws and intellectual property rights is essential. We gotta respect the hard work of others, you know?

Now, let's be upfront about our content. We

gotta make it crystal clear what our stuff is about and any potential risks involved. A solid disclaimer can be our superhero sidekick. Just gotta say our content is for informational or entertainment purposes, not professional advice. Simple as that. It sets expectations straight and minimizes our liability. Nice little safety net, right?

Last but definitely not least, let's create a positive and respectful online community. We don't want things getting out of hand and turning into legal battles, do we? Nah, didn't think so. Encourage constructive conversations, keep an eye on the comments section, and address any issues ASAP. By having clear guidelines and enforcing them consistently, we can keep the peace and avoid unnecessary conflict.

Being a content creator is a pretty sweet gig, but it comes with responsibilities. We can't afford to ignore the legal traps waiting for us. So, let's be smart, my friends. Let's arm ourselves with knowledge and integrity. By being accurate, respecting privacy, and being transparent, we can make sure our creations not only pack a punch but also stay on the right side of the law. It's a balancing act, but hey, we've got this. Time to unleash our creative powers and conquer the legal beast. Let's do it!

STAYING UPDATED ON LEGAL DEVELOPMENTS

So, let me tell you this — if you want to stay in the loop about what's happening in the wild world of legal developments, you've gotta follow the industry experts. These are the folks who live and breathe digital media law, and they're always sharing the inside scoop through blogs, podcasts, social media, and conferences. I mean, keeping an eye on their work is like having your finger on the pulse of the latest legal trends and developments in the content creation game.

Trust me, I've done my fair share of searching for those authoritative voices in the field, and I've found some real gems. These experts know their stuff, from copyright and intellectual property laws to privacy and data protection regulations. By following their work, I've gained the know-how to dodge those legal pitfalls that can trip up content creators like us.

But hey, experts aren't the only place to get your legal fix. Joining legal communities is another game-changer. I'm talking about these communities specially tailored for content creators, where you can rub shoulders with other folks who live at the intersection of law and digital media. And let me tell you, these communities have been a goldmine of information, support, and networking opportunities.

They've got forums, discussion boards, and exclusive content that lets you dive into all kinds of legal issues. It's like having a front-row seat to conversations that matter. And get this — legal professionals often contribute to these communities, so you're not just hearing from fellow content creators, but also getting some wisdom from the experts themselves.

Oh, and don't even get me started on the events these communities organize. We're talking about webinars, workshops, and gatherings that take on the latest legal topics. It's a chance to hear from legal experts firsthand and really get a feel for the legal landscape surrounding content creation. Plus, you get to connect with like-minded individuals who can have your back when things get tricky.

Now, as much as I rely on these industry experts and legal communities, sometimes you just gotta bring in the big guns. Yeah, I'm talking about seeking legal advice from the pros. There have been moments as a content creator when I've come across some seriously complex legal issues that I couldn't figure out on my own. That's when I turned to legal professionals who specialize in this digital media law stuff.

These guys are the real deal. They ensure my work complies with all the legal requirements and keeps me out of any potential legal disputes. Copyright infringement concerns, contracts, new regulations — you name it, they've got the answers. And let me tell you, chatting with these legal pros gives me the confidence and reassurance I need to create content in a way that won't land me in hot water.

Now, finding the right legal professionals isn't always a walk in the park. But luckily, I've got my network in the digital media industry on speed dial. They've been there, done that, and can hook me up with some top-notch recommendations. And when that's not enough, I turn to online directories and platforms that connect content creators with lawyers who really know their stuff.

But here's the kicker — building a relationship with a trusted legal professional is like striking gold. They become your go-to person for timely advice and updates on legal developments that could impact your work. It's that proactive approach that keeps me ahead of any potential legal issues, making sure I'm always on the right side of the law.

So there you have it, my friend. Staying up-to-date on legal developments is no joke in the digital landscape. Following industry experts, joining legal communities, and seeking legal advice when needed have become my secret weapons. They've not only deepened my understanding of all these legal nuances but have also given me a support system that's got my back. Being a content creator means committing to this ongoing journey of staying informed — it's what sets us up for long-term success.

CHAPTER 9

Balancing Creativity and Strategy

DEFINING YOUR CREATIVE VISION

So, when it comes to figuring out what the heck our creative vision is, we gotta start by taking a good long look in the mirror. We gotta dig deep and ask ourselves, "What the heck do I really care about? What gets me fired up? What do I want to shout from the rooftops?" Those answers are gonna be the building blocks of our creative work, the foundation upon which everything else is gonna be built. So, grab a pen and paper, my friends, and start listing down your core values. Is it all about being real and authentic? Is it about showing empathy and understanding? Or maybe you're all about fighting for social justice. Whatever it is, write it down and let those values guide you along this crazy creative journey.

Once we've got those values locked down, we gotta go and check out what other peeps in the creative realm are doing. I mean, let's be real, we all get inspired by somebody or somethin', right? So, it's time to do some good ol' fashioned studying. Immersing ourselves in the work of other creators is gonna give us a boatload of insight into different artistic styles, techniques, and ways of telling stories. But here's the thing, we can't get so caught up in all that inspiration that we forget about our own voice. We gotta stay true to who we are, ya know? So, take a good look at what resonates with you personally. What techniques and elements make your heart sing? Take those bits and pieces and blend 'em into your own work, while still keepin' that distinct creative vision of yours.

Now, let me tell y'all about this little gem I discovered on my own creative journey. It's called a vision board, and it's a freakin' game-changer.

Basically, it's a physical representation of your creative vision. You gather up all these images, quotes, and snippets that align with your values and the kind of content you wanna create. Then, you arrange 'em all pretty-like and stick 'em somewhere you'll see 'em every single day. Trust me, having that vision board in plain sight is gonna keep you inspired, even when doubts and challenges come knocking at your door.

But listen up, folks, defining our creative vision ain't a one-time thing. Nope, it's gonna change and evolve as we change and evolve. So, we gotta stay open to new ideas and experiences. Keep tweaking and reevaluating your creative vision because, hey, we're all a work in progress. We gotta adapt and grow like some badass creative chameleons.

Now, hold tight, 'cause this part is super important. In a world that's bursting at the seams with content, it's gonna be tough AF to stay true to our creative voice. Like, seriously tough. There's gonna be this never-ending pressure to get likes, clicks, and shares. But here's the secret sauce, my friends: remember why you do what you do. Are you here to entertain, educate, inspire, or make people's brains explode with deep thoughts? Whatever your purpose is, use that as your anchor. That's gonna help you filter out all the noise and keep your eyes on the prize - creating content that's true to your unique creative vision.

Oh, and one more thing before I wrap this up. Building a community of like-minded creators is gonna be a total game-changer. I'm talkin' about finding your tribe, the peeps who totally get your values and your vision. These are the people you wanna be having deep conversations with, maybe even collaborate with. They're gonna be your biggest cheerleaders, giving you feedback and pushing you to be the best dang creative you can be. Trust me, having a support system makes all the difference in the world.

Alright, y'all, we're gettin' close to the finish line here. I just gotta give ya one last piece of advice - embrace the freakin' experimentation. Yeah, I know it's scary as hell to step outside our comfort zones, but that's where the magic happens. It's only when we take risks and try new things that our unique creative voices really start to shine. So, give yourself permission to explore new mediums, styles, and topics. Fail a bunch, and then fail some more. 'Cause it's through those failures that we learn and grow, my friends.

To sum it all up, defining our creative vision is a wild roller coaster ride. It's gonna take some serious self-reflection, a healthy dose of inspiration from other creators, and a whole lot of dedication to staying true to our unique selves. But hey, your creative voice is like a freakin' superpower. It's something you gotta cherish, nurture, and let loose on the world through your awesome content. So, keep rockin' it, my fellow creators, and never stop shining!

ANALYZING AUDIENCE EXPECTATIONS

As a content creator, lemme tell ya, understanding what the heck your audience wants is key to making your stuff stick. I mean, what's the point of putting in all this effort if nobody's gonna care, am I right? So, in this chapter, I'll spill the beans on how I've learned to decode audience preferences, pore over viewer feedback, and find that sweet spot between being inventive and giving people what they want.

Now, to get inside the minds of my viewers, I gotta do some serious homework. It ain't enough to churn out stuff that I personally find awesome. At the end of the day, it's all about who's watching. That's why I spend a good chunk of my time diving into demographic data, market trends, and audience behaviors. By sifting through all this juicy info, I get a real clear picture of what my target audience grooves on.

Take this one time when I got obsessed with understanding what gamers dig on YouTube. I went full-on CSI mode, studying popular channels, video views, and all them fancy engagement metrics. And you know what I found? Turns out gamers go gaga over content that's both entertaining and educational. Armed with this treasure trove of info, I tweaked my videos, adding in some smarts while still keeping it fun for my peeps.

But hold up, research alone ain't enough. I gotta get down and dirty with my viewers, talk to 'em like buds. So, I make it a point to ask 'em for feedback, ya know? By encouraging comments and hearing their two cents, I get some insider intel on what they're lovin', hatin', and asking for more of. And trust me, I go through every comment like a detective looking for clues. Not only does that help me suss out what my audience wants, it also builds this rad sense of community with my viewers.

Oh, and don't forget about all them fancy engagement metrics. Likes, dislikes, shares, comments – I watch 'em like a hawk. They give me a clear idea of how my content's hitting home. If a particular type of video's getting mad love, with tons of likes and positive comments, I know I'm on the right track. But if it's getting thumbs down or negative vibes, I know I gotta switch it up and make some improvements. It's like a constant dance, ya know? I'm always trying to please my crowd and give 'em what they want.

Here's the thing though, I can't be a complete

pushover to audience feedback. Gotta spice things up and keep 'em guessing. That's where creative experimentation comes in, my friend. If I just stick to what people expect, it'll get boring real quick. So, I go wild and try out new ideas. But hey, I do it with caution, ya know? Gotta make sure I'm still in tune with my audience.

When I'm ready to give something new a go, I start with releasing a pilot video, sorta like a tester. Then, I pay close attention to what my viewers gotta say about it. If the response is off the charts, I know I'm onto something and start finessing the concept. But if it's not hitting home like I hoped, I take a step back, reevaluate, and make it better.

To find that perfect balance, I also make sure to keep my viewers in the loop. I let 'em know about my wild experiments and give 'em a chance to share their thoughts. I mean, communication is key, right? By being open and transparent, I build trust with my audience and manage their expectations. It's like a secret ingredient to keeping everyone happy and invested in what I do.

So, to sum it all up, knowing what makes your audience tick, listening to their feedback, and treading that fine line between creativity and expectations are vital for any content creator. With solid research, engaging with your viewers, and a cautious approach to experimenting, you can hit that sweet spot where your content speaks to your peeps while still pushing boundaries. And trust me, it's totally worth it when you've got a loyal crew cheering you on.

EMBRACING MARKET TRENDS

Alright, let's talk about embracing market trends without selling out your artistic soul. Finding that sweet spot between staying true to your vision and jumping on the bandwagon isn't always easy, but it's definitely possible. Trust me, I've been there.

Let me introduce you to Olivia, a brilliant filmmaker who was all about making thought-provoking documentaries that packed a punch. But she started noticing a shift in the content landscape.

Short-form videos were taking over platforms like TikTok and Instagram Reels, and Olivia couldn't help but be curious about what all the fuss was about.

At first, Olivia was a bit hesitant to dive head-first into this new trend. She was afraid that the depth and complexity of her storytelling would be compromised. But you know what they say, fortune favors the bold. So instead of pushing the trend away, she decided to dig deeper and under-stand why it was gaining so much popularity.

Olivia realized that short-form videos were like bite-sized snacks for our fast-paced digital lives. People wanted easily digestible content that fit their on-the-go lifestyle. This revelation sparked some-thing in her, and she saw an opportunity to adapt her storytelling skills to this emerging trend.

She began her journey by immersing herself in these short-form videos, meticulously analyz-ing what made them tick. She deconstructed the storytelling techniques, editing styles, and visual strategies that captivated audiences in just a few minutes. And the more she delved into this world, the more she realized that she could still tell compelling stories, even within the constraints of a shorter format.

Armed with this newfound knowledge, Olivia decided to take some risks. She started creating teasers for her upcoming documentaries, capturing the essence of her larger work in just a few captivating moments. These teasers left her audience wanting more, keeping them hooked and hungry. By incorporating engaging visuals and concise storytelling techniques, Olivia created a sense of anticipation and curiosity.

But Olivia wasn't content with just riding the trend wave. She knew that trends come and go faster than you can say "viral." So she made it a habit to scroll through various social media platforms every day, keeping an eye on what other creators were doing and noting the emerging trends. It wasn't about copying what others were doing, but rather understanding the underlying principles and ideas driving those trends.

Olivia engaged with her audience, sought feedback, and embraced their suggestions. She made her viewers feel like she was on their wavelength, evolving with them and adapting to their ever-changing tastes. This connection she built with her audience allowed her to create content that was not just relevant but also meaningful.

Embracing market trends isn't about blindly following what's popular, but about understanding the shift in society, tastes, and technology. By recognizing and leveraging the motivations behind these trends, content creators can create work that resonates. Olivia's journey is one that many of us face – the never-ending quest to balance artistry with market demands. It's a constant process of exploration, experimentation, and evolution.

To navigate this balancing act, content creators need to see trends as tools in their creative arsenal. Just like a painter experimenting with new brushes or a writer exploring different literary techniques, we can use trends to enhance our storytelling. By being proactive and informed, we shape trends instead of letting them dictate our work. We mold them to fit our unique aesthetic and vision.

So my friends, embrace those market trends. It's the key to connecting deeply with your audience while staying true to your artistic integrity. But remember, this isn't a one-and-done deal. It's an ongoing process of staying open-minded, adaptable, and eager to learn. And by doing so, we can thrive in the ever-changing digital landscape, captivate audiences, and create content that stands the test of time.

THE ROLE OF ANALYTICS AND DATA

As a content creator, let me tell you, data and analytics are like the secret weapons in my content strategy arsenal. Now, I always knew they were important, but it wasn't until recently that I had this epiphany about just how powerful they really are. Seriously, they can do some pretty magical stuff. In this chapter, I'm gonna spill the beans on how analytics and data can totally transform your content creation game. Get ready for a wild ride!

Let's start with tracking audience engagement. This is where the real gold is, my friend. With the right tools and platforms, you can dive deep into the minds of your audience and see what makes 'em tick. I've used all kinds of metrics like page views, bounce rates, click-through rates, and time on page to figure out what content my audience is eating up. It's like being a detective on a mission to crack the code of their preferences and interests.

One tool that's been an absolute game-changer for me is Google Analytics. Man, I can't even begin to describe the treasure trove of insights it provides. By slapping a tracking code onto my website, I can unlock detailed reports on everything from user demographics to their actual behavior on my site. It's like having x-ray vision into their online lives! Armed with all this juicy data, I can spot patterns and trends quicker than a cheetah chasing its prey. If I see that my audience is devouring articles on personal finance, you bet your sweet bippy I'm gonna create more content in that niche. It's like giving them exactly what they want, when they want it.

Now, tracking audience engagement is just the tip of the iceberg. Hold onto your seat because things are about to get even more intense. Brace yourself for the mind-bending world of analyzing content performance. This is where we find out if our content is hitting the bullseye or falling flat on its face. And let me tell you, it's like riding a roller-coaster of emotions.

Social media platforms like Facebook Insights and Twitter Analytics are like my trusty sidekicks in this adventure. They spill the beans on how well my content is doing in terms of reach and engagement. I can see which posts are getting all the love, the comments, and the shares. It's like getting a pat on the back from my audience in real-time! And the best part? I can figure out what content performs best on each platform, like figuring out the secret sauce to each social media recipe. With all this insider knowledge, I can fine-tune my social media strategy and make sure my content is hitting its mark.

But wait, there's more! I also keep a close eye on what impact my content is having on search engine rankings. Yeah, that's right, I'm playing in the big leagues now. Tools like Google Search Console and SEMrush are my secret weapons here. I can track the organic traffic generated by my content and find out what keywords are driving people to my website. It's like having my very own SEO superpower. Armed with this info, I can tweak my SEO strategy and make my content more visible to search engines. It's like being the puppet master of the internet.

Alright, take a deep breath because we've almost reached the end of this journey. So, now that we've collected all this mind-blowing data, what do we do with it? Well, my friend, we leverage it like a pro. Data-driven insights are like a treasure map leading us to success. They provide invaluable guidance on what content topics, formats, and distribution channels will blow your audience's minds.

For instance, let's say I dive into the social media engagement data and discover that my audience freakin' loves video content. That's my cue to go all-in on videos, baby. I'll prioritize creating more of that jaw-dropping video content and throw my resources at it like it's the last piece of pizza. Plus, data analytics can help me spot gaps in my content strategy like a hawk spots a mouse. If I uncover keywords I haven't targeted yet, you can bet your bottom dollar I'll create content to fill those gaps and reel in a wider audience.

Last but not least, data analytics gives me the power to make killer decisions on content promotion and distribution. It's like having a crystal ball that shows me exactly where my audience is hanging out and what makes 'em tick. Armed with this insider knowledge, I can focus my promotional efforts on those platforms that really get their engines revving. It's like being a mastermind strategist, always one step ahead of the game.

So there you have it, my friend. The role of analytics and data in content creation is like having a magical compass that leads us straight to success. It's like peering into a crystal ball and seeing exactly what our audience wants and needs. It's like having a secret playbook that helps us create content that resonates on a whole new level. In this crazy world of content creation, analytics and data are our not-so-secret weapons, our superpower. So grab your cape and let's conquer this content creation universe together!

EXPERIMENTATION AND EVOLUTION

You know, there's something magical about diving into the unknown, testing the boundaries, and uncovering new ideas. It's like embarking on a thrilling adventure where creativity is the compass and innovation is the destination. As content creators, we're driven by this insatiable thirst for pushing the limits and crafting something that's truly one-of-a-kind.

But let's talk real talk here. One thing I've learned on this wild rollercoaster ride is that failure is inevitable. And you know what? It's not a bad thing. In fact, it's something to be celebrated. Failure is like a secret passage to growth and learning.

Each stumble brings us closer to success, teaching us resilience and determination.

When we pick ourselves up from a failure, it forces us to reevaluate our strategies, learn from our blunders, and get to know ourselves better. It's like a crash course in self-awareness. By embracing failure, we become these unstoppable forces ready to take on the unpredictable world of content creation.

But let me tell you something, my friend. This journey isn't just about us creators. It's about our audience too. Yes, they hold the key to the kingdom. Our ultimate goal is to connect with them, captivate their attention, and create content that speaks to their very souls. So we need to listen. We need to pay attention to their ever-changing preferences and adapt our content accordingly.

Audience preferences? Oh, they're like quicksilver, always shifting and changing. So it's up to us to keep our antennae up, be open-minded, and actively seek their feedback. We've got to pay close attention to the data and metrics that show us how our content is performing. It's through this understanding that we can serve up the content that they crave and make a lasting impact.

And hey, if we want to stay on top of our game, we've got to stay ahead of the curve. In this saturated world of content creation, it's not enough to just go with the flow. We've got to be willing to adapt and evolve. Trends come and go, my friend, and those who are willing to bend with them will rise above the noise.

In my own journey, I've learned that embracing experimentation and continuous evolution is like sprouting wings and flying. It's exhilarating and transformational. It's breaking free from the chains of tradition, defying expectations, and blazing our own trails. Through pushing those creative boundaries, I've discovered passions I never knew I had and grown in ways I couldn't imagine.

But let me tell you, it ain't all sunshine and rainbows. Experimentation and evolution require guts, grit, and unwavering self-belief. We've got to trust our instincts, follow our passions, and take risks even when the outcome is uncertain. It's through these challenges that we truly grow, becoming the best damn content creators we can be.

So my fellow content creators, let's embrace this call to experiment and evolve. Let's push our creative limits, learn from our failures, and adapt to our audience's ever-changing desires. It's through this process that we'll discover our unique voices and make a lasting impact in the vast world of content creation. So go forth, my friends, fearlessly explore the uncharted waters of creativity. The possibilities are endless, and the rewards? Well, let me tell you, they're beyond measure.

THE ROLE OF ANALYTICS AND DATA

As a content creator, let me tell you, data and analytics are like the secret weapons in my content strategy arsenal. Now, I always knew they were important, but it wasn't until recently that I had this epiphany about just how powerful they really are. Seriously, they can do some pretty magical stuff.

In this chapter, I'm gonna spill the beans on how analytics and data can totally transform your content creation game. Get ready for a wild ride!

Let's start with tracking audience engagement. This is where the real gold is, my friend. With the right tools and platforms, you can dive deep into the minds of your audience and see what makes 'em tick. I've used all kinds of metrics like page views, bounce rates, click-through rates, and time on page to figure out what content my audience is eating up. It's like being a detective on a mission to crack the code of their preferences and interests.

One tool that's been an absolute game-changer for me is Google Analytics. Man, I can't even begin to describe the treasure trove of insights it provides. By slapping a tracking code onto my website, I can unlock detailed reports on everything from user demographics to their actual behavior on my site. It's like having x-ray vision into their online lives! Armed with all this juicy data, I can spot patterns and trends quicker than a cheetah chasing its prey. If I see that my audience is devouring articles on personal finance, you bet your sweet bippy I'm gonna create more content in that niche. It's like giving them exactly what they want, when they want it.

Now, tracking audience engagement is just the tip of the iceberg. Hold onto your seat because things are about to get even more intense. Brace yourself for the mind-bending world of analyzing content performance. This is where we find out if our content is hitting the bullseye or falling flat on its face. And let me tell you, it's like riding a roller-coaster of emotions.

Social media platforms like Facebook Insights and Twitter Analytics are like my trusty sidekicks in this adventure. They spill the beans on how well my content is doing in terms of reach and engagement. I can see which posts are getting all the love, the comments, and the shares. It's like getting a pat on the back from my audience in real-time! And the best part? I can figure out what content performs best on each platform, like figuring out the secret sauce to each social media recipe. With all this insider knowledge, I can fine-tune my social media strategy and make sure my content is hitting its mark.

But wait, there's more! I also keep a close eye on what impact my content is having on search engine rankings. Yeah, that's right, I'm playing in the big leagues now. Tools like Google Search Console and SEMrush are my secret weapons here. I can track the organic traffic generated by my content and find out what keywords are driving people to my website. It's like having my very own SEO superpower. Armed with this info, I can tweak my SEO strategy and make my content more visible to search engines. It's like being the puppet master of the internet.

Alright, take a deep breath because we've almost reached the end of this journey. So, now that we've collected all this mind-blowing data, what do we do with it? Well, my friend, we leverage it like a pro. Data-driven insights are like a treasure map leading us to success. They provide invaluable guidance on what content topics, formats, and distribution channels will blow your audience's minds.

For instance, let's say I dive into the social media engagement data and discover that my audience freakin' loves video content. That's my cue to go all-in on videos, baby. I'll prioritize creating more of that jaw-dropping video content and throw my resources at it like it's the last piece of pizza. Plus, data analytics can help me spot gaps in my content strategy like a hawk spots a mouse. If I uncover keywords I haven't targeted yet, you can bet your bottom dollar I'll create content to fill those gaps and reel in a wider audience.

Last but not least, data analytics gives me the power to make killer decisions on content promotion and distribution. It's like having a crystal ball that shows me exactly where my audience is hanging out and what makes 'em tick. Armed with this insider knowledge, I can focus my promotional efforts on those platforms that really get their engines revving. It's like being a mastermind strategist, always one step ahead of the game.

So there you have it, my friend. The role of analytics and data in content creation is like having a magical compass that leads us straight to success.

It's like peering into a crystal ball and seeing exactly what our audience wants and needs. It's like having a secret playbook that helps us create content that resonates on a whole new level. In this crazy world of content creation, analytics and data are our not-so-secret weapons, our superpower. So grab your cape and let's conquer this content creation universe together!

EXPERIMENTATION AND EVOLUTION

You know, there's something magical about diving into the unknown, testing the boundaries, and uncovering new ideas. It's like embarking on a thrilling adventure where creativity is the compass and innovation is the destination. As content creators, we're driven by this insatiable thirst for pushing the limits and crafting something that's truly one-of-a-kind.

But let's talk real talk here. One thing I've learned on this wild rollercoaster ride is that failure is inevitable. And you know what? It's not a bad thing. In fact, it's something to be celebrated. Failure is like a secret passage to growth and learning. Each stumble brings us closer to success, teaching us resilience and determination.

When we pick ourselves up from a failure, it forces us to reevaluate our strategies, learn from our blunders, and get to know ourselves better. It's like a crash course in self-awareness. By embracing failure, we become these unstoppable forces ready to take on the unpredictable world of content creation.

But let me tell you something, my friend. This journey isn't just about us creators. It's about our audience too. Yes, they hold the key to the kingdom. Our ultimate goal is to connect with them, captivate their attention, and create content that speaks to their very souls. So we need to listen. We need to pay attention to their ever-changing preferences and adapt our content accordingly.

Audience preferences? Oh, they're like quicksilver, always shifting and changing. So it's up to us to keep our antennae up, be open-minded, and actively seek their feedback. We've got to pay close attention to the data and metrics that show us how our content is performing. It's through this understanding that we can serve up the content that they crave and make a lasting impact.

And hey, if we want to stay on top of our game, we've got to stay ahead of the curve. In this saturated world of content creation, it's not enough to just go with the flow. We've got to be willing to adapt and evolve. Trends come and go, my friend, and those who are willing to bend with them will rise above the noise.

In my own journey, I've learned that embracing experimentation and continuous evolution is like sprouting wings and flying. It's exhilarating and transformational. It's breaking free from the chains of tradition, defying expectations, and blazing our own trails. Through pushing those creative boundaries, I've discovered passions I never knew I had and grown in ways I couldn't imagine.

But let me tell you, it ain't all sunshine and rainbows. Experimentation and evolution require guts, grit, and unwavering self-belief. We've got to trust our instincts, follow our passions, and take risks even when the outcome is uncertain. It's through these challenges that we truly grow, becoming the best damn content creators we can be.

So my fellow content creators, let's embrace this call to experiment and evolve. Let's push our creative limits, learn from our failures, and adapt to our audience's ever-changing desires. It's through this process that we'll discover our unique voices and make a lasting impact in the vast world of content creation. So go forth, my friends, fearlessly explore the uncharted waters of creativity. The possibilities are endless, and the rewards? Well, let me tell you, they're beyond measure.

CHAPTER 10

Building Authentic Connections

THE POWER OF AUTHENTICITY

So, picture this: you're scrolling through your social media feed, and it's like a content tsunami out there. Everywhere you look, there's someone trying to catch your attention, trying to make you stop and pay heed. It's crazy, really. With millions of creators battling it out, it's hard to stand out from the noise. But hey, don't stress, because I've got the secret to making your mark.

You see, it all boils down to one word: authenticity. Trust me, I know. When I first embarked on my journey as a content creator, I was all about that perfectly curated image. I spent hours meticulously editing and filtering my content, making sure it looked picture-perfect. But here's the thing: I didn't realize that by doing that, I was depriving my audience of something real, something they could truly connect with.

It wasn't until I decided to drop the act, to show my vulnerable side, that I experienced a mind-blowing shift in audience engagement. The more I let my true self shine through, flaws and all, the more my audience responded. Suddenly, they could see the real me, and they appreciated that authenticity more than anything.

You know what the researchers say? Vulnerability builds trust, baby. When we content creators open up and share our fears, our insecurities, our struggles, it creates a safe space for our audience to do the same. It's all about empathy and relatability. It's like we're saying, "Hey, I'm not perfect. I'm just like you, dealing with all this messy stuff called life."

But here's the thing: vulnerability on its own ain't enough. Nope, transparency is just as important. See, when we content creators peel back the curtain and let our audience see the behind-the-scenes process, the failures and the successes, we're giving them a front-row seat to our authentic journey. We're saying, "Look, I've got nothing to hide. This is me, real and raw." And that makes us more human. More relatable. More approachable.

I can vouch for this firsthand. The more transparent I am about my creative process, the more my audience gets hooked. They love it when I share my failed attempts, my struggles, or those aha moments that change everything. They feel like they're on this crazy ride with me, invested in my success and growth.

But guess what? Building a dedicated fan base isn't just about vulnerability and transparency. Nope, it's also about forging genuine connections. Our audience is our lifeline, my friend. They're the ones who consume and share our content, who have our backs through thick and thin. So it's crucial to nurture those relationships and make them count.

I make a point to engage with my audience on a personal level. I respond to their comments and messages, take the time to understand their needs and preferences, and you bet I incorporate their feedback into my content. I want them to know that their opinion matters, and that they're an essential part of my creative journey.

Now, here's another trick I've learned: collaborating with other creators is a game-changer. When I team up with someone I genuinely admire, it's like a magical exchange of ideas and exposure. These collaborations not only expand my network, but they also give my audience a taste of different perspectives and experiences.

So, here's the bottom line: authenticity is the real deal in content creation. When we embrace vulnerability, transparency, and genuine connections, we create a fan base that's passionately invested in our journey. Yeah, it takes courage to let go of that perfect facade and show our true colors. But trust me, the rewards are beyond measure. So ditch that mask, my friend, and embrace that raw, unfiltered you. That's where true connection lies.

CONNECTING WITH YOUR AUDIENCE

Alright, so let's talk about something super important for us content creators: making a real connection with our audience. I mean, they're the ones who keep coming back, engaging with our stuff, and ultimately, making us successful. In this chapter, we're gonna dive into some practical techniques to really connect with our viewers on a deeper level. We're gonna learn how to have meaningful conversations, why it's crucial to respond to comments, and how to create content that hits 'em right in the feels.

First up, let's talk about engaging in these meaningful conversations. Look, gone are the days when we could just create content and not interact with our viewers. Nowadays, they want that interaction, that engagement. They wanna feel like they're part of our journey. So, to get those conversations going, try using these strategies:

Number one, ask some thought-provoking questions. I'm not talking about basic, surface-level stuff here. Go deep, dig into those emotions, and get their critical thinking gears turning. Your goal is to make 'em really think and get 'em to share their thoughts and experiences. You want that real connection, right?

Number two, respond like lightning. When someone takes the time to comment on your content, don't leave 'em hanging. Respond as soon as you can, and be authentic about it. Show 'em that you value their input and appreciate their engagement. Use their comments to keep the conversation going and make sure they know you hear 'em.

Last but not least, create content that brings people together. You gotta foster that sense of community among your viewers. Try coming up with challenges or contests that get 'em actively involved. By making 'em an integral part of your content creation process, you'll build a stronger connection and create a supportive community of like-minded folks.

Now, let's talk about responding to comments. Look, comments can make or break us as content creators, right? So, it's not enough to just respond, we gotta do it in a way that really means something. Here are some techniques to help ya out:

First off, show genuine appreciation. Seriously, when someone takes the time to comment, let 'em know you're grateful. Thank 'em for watching, engaging, and sharing their thoughts. Not only will this encourage further engagement, but it'll also make people think highly of you as a content creator.

Next, address comments individually. Forget those copy-paste responses, alright? Take the time to really consider each comment and respond individually. This shows that you care about what they have to say and are committed to building that personal connection. Let 'em know you heard 'em and value their thoughts by addressing their specific points or questions.

And finally, encourage more dialogue. Don't just end the conversation with one response. Keep it goin' by asking follow-up questions or seeking additional input. This back-and-forth exchange fosters a stronger bond with your audience. By actively participating in these conversations, you show 'em that you're all about building real relationships.

Okay, now let's get into the nitty-gritty of creating emotionally resonant content. We all know emotions have serious power when it comes to connecting with our audience. So, here are a few techniques to really tug at those heartstrings:

First things first, you gotta understand your audience. Take the time to figure out what they want, what they need, and what interests 'em. Do some research, run surveys, or even reach out directly. The more you know, the better you can tailor your content to evoke the exact emotional response you're after.

Next up, storytelling. This is a secret weapon,

my friends. Share personal stories, experiences, or even interview others to give your viewers a little taste of real life. When you tell authentic stories, you give 'em something relatable, something that hits 'em right in the gut and creates that emotional bond we're after.

And finally, try to evoke empathy and inspiration. These are two powerful emotions that can really connect you with your audience. Make content that brings out joy, sadness, motivation - whatever emotion you want 'em to feel. Talk about universal themes and emotions that they can relate to. This kind of connection goes beyond the digital realm and sticks with 'em.

So, here's the deal. Connecting with your audience is more than just uploading content. It's about stirring up engagement, having those meaningful conversations, and creating content that hits 'em right in the feels. By using these techniques, you'll forge a deeper connection with your viewers and build a loyal and engaged audience. Remember, it's all about being authentic, empathetic, and genuinely wanting to connect with 'em on a meaningful level.

CULTIVATING RELATIONSHIPS WITH FELLOW CREATORS

So, you wanna know how to build supportive relationships with other creators? Well, one of the first steps is to actively seek out collaboration opportunities. Trust me, when you team up with fellow creators, it's like combining a bunch of superpowers. You exchange ideas, skills, and expertise, and that's just the beginning.

Collaboration not only helps you expand your audience and reach, but it's also a chance for fantastic synergy to happen. It's like a fusion of talent and perspectives, a creative explosion of greatness.

To find potential collaborators, do your research! Jump into different online platforms, like social media, video-sharing websites, and content creator forums, to discover like-minded individuals who create content similar to yours. Look for those who share your vision and are dedicated to producing high-quality stuff.

Once you've found potential collaborators, it's time to make the first move. Don't be shy! Reach out through direct messaging, email, or even commenting on their content. Be genuine and sincere, expressing your admiration for their work and explaining how collaborating would benefit both of you. Show that you're enthusiastic and committed to working together.

Don't forget about networking events and industry conferences! These gatherings are gold mines for building relationships with fellow creators. You'll have the chance to showcase your work, participate in panel discussions, and attend workshops and seminars. It's a whirlwind of inspiration and knowledge, and you can connect with other passionate content creators.

Prepare yourself for these events. Have business cards or other promotional materials ready to share with potential collaborators or industry professionals. Be actively engaged in discussions, talk to people, and make memorable interactions. You never know what could come out of these connections – future collaborations or partnerships might be just around the corner.

While seeking collaboration opportunities and attending events are crucial, don't forget about fostering a sense of community within the industry. Community is everything! It gives you support, encouragement, and a source of inspiration to keep going.

To foster that sense of community, consider creating or joining online groups or communities specifically for content creators. These groups are a safe space to connect with like-minded individuals, share resources, ask for advice, and celebrate successes. They can be found on social media platforms or specialized forums and websites.

Within these communities, you get to engage in discussions, offer constructive feedback, and collaborate on cool projects. You can also organize virtual or in-person meetups and events. It's a chance for creators to come together to network, share experiences, and learn from one another. It's a support system that ensures you're never alone in your journey.

But here's an extra secret: don't just focus on yourself – support and promote fellow creators too. Share their content with your audience, give them shoutouts on social media, or even collaborate on joint projects. By actively uplifting others, you contribute to a positive and nurturing community where everyone can thrive.

To wrap it all up, cultivating relationships with other creators is a game-changer. It opens doors to collaboration opportunities, networking events, and a sense of belonging. So, go out there and actively seek collaboration, attend industry events, and foster that amazing sense of community. We're all in this together, and when we work hand in hand, we create a thriving and vibrant industry.

EMBRACING VULNERABILITY

You know, one of the most powerful things

about being a content creator is that it allows you to tap into this well of vulnerability. It's like this endless resource of stories, experiences, and perspectives that are uniquely ours. And let me tell you, when we embrace that vulnerability, something magical happens. Our content not only connects with others, but it also has the power to inspire and heal.

But, man, it's not always easy to put ourselves out there. We live in a society that values perfection and masks vulnerability like it's some kind of weakness. So, it's natural to feel intimidated and afraid of what others might think when we start sharing our personal stories. But here's the thing - vulnerability is not a weakness. It's a strength. It takes guts to expose our vulnerabilities and fears, but the rewards are beyond measure.

I remember when I first started as a content creator. I was so scared to reveal too much of my personal life. I mean, what would my audience think

Would they see me as weak or flawed? It was a constant battle in my head. But as I dove deeper into the creative process, I had a realization. Vulnerability is what makes our content resonate. It's what sets us apart from the rest, because no one else has lived our unique narrative.

When we share our triumphs, struggles, and lessons learned, we invite others into our world. We show them that they are not alone in their ups and downs. We create a bond of understanding and empathy that encourages others to embrace their own vulnerability and share their stories too. It's this beautiful cycle of connection and growth.

But there's something that holds so many of us back - the fear of judgment. We worry that if we reveal our true selves, others will see us as inadequate or flawed. And let me tell you, that fear is real. There will always be people out there who disagree or find fault with our work. That's just the nature of the game. But embracing vulnerability means accepting that judgment is part of the process and not letting it stop us from expressing ourselves.

Now, here's the key to overcoming that fear - shifting our perspective. Instead of seeking validation from others, we need to learn to validate ourselves. We have to trust in our own experiences and the value they hold. When we focus on creating content that is authentic and genuine, we attract an audience that resonates with our message. The ones who truly get us will appreciate our vulnerability, while the others just won't be our target audience. And that's okay.

The beauty of embracing vulnerability is in the authentic connections we create. When we open ourselves up and share our truth, we give others permission to do the same. And when our content resonates with someone on a deeper level, it sparks conversations and fosters growth. We create a safe space where people feel comfortable sharing their own vulnerabilities. And let me tell you, that's where the magic happens.

I remember this one moment that stayed with me as a content creator. A viewer reached out to me to share her personal story. She told me how my vulnerability had inspired her to confront her own fears and start sharing her journey too. And that, my friends, is the power of vulnerability.

Through our genuine self-expression, we have the ability to help others find the strength and courage to embrace their own vulnerabilities. It's a truly remarkable feeling.

So, my dear content creators, I urge you to embrace your vulnerability. Share your personal stories, face your fears head-on, and create those authentic connections through genuine self-expression. Your vulnerability is not a weakness, it's your superpower. And by harnessing it, you have the power to create content that not only impacts lives but also changes them. Trust me, it's through vulnerability that we find our true selves and leave an indelible mark on the world.

NURTURING A DEDICATED FAN BASE

So, let's talk about something near and dear to my heart: fan contributions. I mean, without those amazing folks showing their support and getting engaged, where would we be? They're the reason I wake up every morning excited to create more content. And let me tell you, I've found some pretty awesome ways to show them just how much I appreciate them.

First things first, it's all about those regular interactions. Taking the time to respond to comments on social media or giving shoutouts and thank you's in my videos, it's all part of making those personal connections. And let me tell you, when my fans feel recognized, their loyalty only grows stronger.

But what about giveaways and contests? Oh yeah, those things work like magic. I love running contests where fans have the chance to win exclusive merch or behind-the-scenes experiences. It gets my fans pumped up and motivated to spread the word about my content. It's a win-win situation, really. They get something cool, and I get to expand my fan base.

Now, let's move on to fan events. These babies are the real deal. When I organize these shindigs, it's like witnessing the birth of a community. I make sure to plan activities that help my fans connect with each other, like group discussions and creative workshops. And let's not forget the cosplay competitions - those are always a blast. Honestly, these events bring fans together and tighten their bonds, not just with me, but with each other.

But the best part? Fan events give me a chance to get up close and personal with my fans. Whether it's a meet-and-greet or Q&A panel, I get to show them the person behind the content. And let me tell you, when fans can put a face to the name, it builds trust and a deeper emotional connection. That's the kind of connection that keeps them coming back for more.

And speaking of exclusive content, let me tell you, it's a game-changer. By offering content that's not available to the general public, I'm giving fans a reason to really step up and become dedicated supporters. I do this through a tiered subscription model where each level offers its own special perks and exclusive content. It's like a choose-your-own-adventure, where fans get to pick their level of support and feel appreciated for it.

But I don't stop there. I also involve my dedicated supporters directly in the creation process. I'm talking collaborations, where they get the chance to be featured in my videos or podcasts, or even be part of a live show. I want them to feel special and proud of being part of my journey. And let me tell you, it works like a charm. It's a win-win situation yet again.

So, to sum it all up, building a dedicated fan base is all about recognition, appreciation, and engagement. By recognizing and appreciating fan contributions, organizing fan events that create a sense of community, and creating exclusive content for the die-hard supporters, I've been able to cultivate a fan base that's not just loyal, but passionate too. And let me tell you, that kind of connection and positive word-of-mouth is what keeps me going and growing as a content creator.

CHAPTER 11

The Future of Content Creation

THE RISE OF VIRTUAL REALITY

I still remember that warm summer day when I first dove into the virtual world. The headset clung to my head, totally enveloping me in a completely new dimension. It was like nothing I had ever experienced before. The pixels shifted and transformed into breathtaking landscapes right before my eyes, while the sounds of the virtual realm wrapped around me, immersing me even further. This wasn't just some technological upgrade; it was a freaking portal into a whole new world of content creation.

In the past, content creators were stuck with traditional two-dimensional mediums like print, film, and photography. Don't get me wrong, those mediums had their own charm, but virtual reality blew them out of the water. It broke free from the constraints of a flat screen and brought storytelling into a fully interactive three-dimensional environment. The possibilities were endless and practically unexplored, with the potential to turn storytelling, gaming, and interactive entertainment on their heads.

Let's talk about storytelling for a sec. As a writer, I'm a sucker for the power of a good story. Whether it's in novels, films, or even social media posts, stories have this magical ability to whisk us off to different worlds and make us feel all the feels. But you know what virtual reality did? It took storytelling to a whole new level, man. With this technology, audiences didn't just sit on the sidelines anymore. Nah, they became active participants, like they were smack dab in the middle of the story.

Imagine strolling through the halls of Hogwarts or wandering through the vast landscapes of Middle-Earth. With virtual reality, those dreams became a freaking reality, dude. Creators weren't restricted to just describing worlds anymore; they could actually build them from scratch and invite audiences to be a part of it all. Talk about stepping into the pages of a book, right?

Now let's shift gears and chat about gaming. The gaming industry has always been on the frontline of technological innovation, from crappy pixelated graphics to the mind-blowing realism we've got today. Virtual reality didn't just throw a new toy at the gaming industry; it opened up a whole new playground for them to mess around in.

Virtual reality gaming was like nothing you'd ever experienced, man. Say goodbye to traditional controllers and say hello to intuitive hand and body tracking systems. You could physically engage with the virtual environment, dude. It wasn't just about up, down, left, and right anymore – it was about actually feeling the weight of the sword in your hand and getting a rush of adrenaline in your veins. Virtual reality changed the game, blurring the line between what's real and what's not. It was like jumping headfirst into a world of pure imagination.

But here's the thing, virtual reality wasn't just about storytelling and gaming. Oh no, it had the potential to shake up the whole interactive entertainment scene and bridge the gap between reality and virtual reality. Take education for example. The old school way of learning had textbooks and boring lectures, but virtual reality turned learning into this immersive, hands-on experience. You could explore historical sites, conduct scientific experiments, and heck, even travel through time, all from the comfort of a virtual reality headset. Now that's some next-level stuff, my friend.

And it doesn't stop there. Virtual reality had applications in fields like healthcare, architecture, and tourism. Surgeons could use virtual reality simulations to train without the risks. Architects could give clients a virtual tour of what their designs would look like before they even broke ground. And travelers? They could explore new destinations without ever leaving their couch. It was like bringing the world to your living room.

The future of interactive entertainment was a wild ride, man. Virtual reality was seamlessly merging both physical and virtual realities, blurring the lines between them. As content creators, it was up to us to harness the true potential of virtual reality, to push the boundaries of what was possible, and to blow people's minds. We were on the cusp of something huge, and we needed to take that leap into the unknown.

So, in conclusion, virtual reality was a game-changer for content creation. It took us out of the two-dimensional box and thrust us into a fully interactive, three-dimensional wonderland. Story-telling became more immersive, gaming became more physical, and the world of interactive entertainment was forever transformed. The journey had just begun, my friend, and with each new innovation, the possibilities continued to expand. We had a responsibility to uncover the untold secrets of virtual reality and bring them to light. And man, was it gonna be one hell of a ride.

THE INFLUENCE OF ARTIFICIAL INTELLIGENCE

So, it's crazy to think about how artificial intelligence has become such a big part of our lives, especially when it comes to content creation. I mean, have you ever wondered how those articles, blog posts, or YouTube videos magically appear in your feed, perfectly tailored to your interests?

Well, let me tell you, it's all thanks to AI. This fascinating technology is not only capable of generating content on its own but also predicting what you'll like based on your online behavior. It's like having a personal concierge who knows you better than you know yourself.

But of course, with great power comes great responsibility. We can't talk about AI in content creation without addressing the ethical dilemmas it presents. It's a double-edged sword, really.

On one hand, AI-generated content opens up

a whole new world of possibilities. It can churn out articles at lightning speed, saving us time and energy. But on the other hand, it poses a threat to human creativity. Are we slowly being replaced by machines? Will our unique perspectives and voices become obsolete?

And then there are the personalized recommendations. It's both exhilarating and unnerving to know that an AI algorithm can predict our preferences and cater to our every whim. It's like having a genie that knows our deepest desires. But at the same time, this kind of personalization can create an echo chamber, trapping us in a bubble of limited perspectives and reinforcing our biases.

It's a constant battle between convenience and authenticity, efficiency and originality. As consumers, we are torn between enjoying the seamless experience AI provides and questioning the underlying motives of these AI-driven platforms.

But hey, that's the world we live in now. The line between human and machine is becoming increasingly blurred, and it's up to us to navigate this brave new world. So, enjoy the content, embrace the recommendations, but never forget to take a step back, think critically, and question the influence of AI in shaping our online experiences.

EVOLVING PLATFORMS AND FORMATS

Alright, let's kickstart this journey by diving into the wild world of short-form videos. We're talking TikTok, Instagram Reels, and YouTube Shorts - the holy trinity of bite-sized storytelling. These little nuggets of content have turned the content creation scene on its head, capturing the elusive attention of a generation notorious for their rapidly disappearing attention spans. Clocking in at just a few seconds to a minute, these quickfire vids offer an immersive experience that's easy on the eyes and brain. They give us a sneak peek into the lives of content creators, all packaged up in a shiny, visually appealing format. And speaking as a content creator myself, let me tell you, these short videos are like rocket fuel for building a die-hard fanbase and creating your own brand. By adapting my content to fit the vibe of these platforms, I've seen my engagement and reach skyrocket, connecting with a wider audience and nurturing a thriving community.

Now, let's shift gears and enter the realm of live streaming. Picture yourself immersed in a world where authenticity reigns supreme. Platforms like Twitch, YouTube Live, and Facebook Live have revolutionized the way content creators interact with their audience. It's the real deal, folks. This is where the magic happens - genuine, real-time connections. Live streaming lets creators flaunt their skills, share their passions, and build bonds with viewers scattered across the globe. But here's where it gets interesting: through the chat feature, creators can feel the pulse of their audience, responding to comments, questions, and suggestions on the spot. It's like having a direct line to the people who adore your content. This dynamic form of content creation creates a sense of community, generating a loyal following of folks who feel like they're a part of something bigger - a tight-knit crew united by the creator and their craft. Whether you're gaming, whipping up some grub, or simply shooting the breeze, live streaming takes content creation to dizzying heights of interactivity.

But wait, there's more. Let's take a detour and explore the enigmatic world of podcasts. My friends, get ready to be transported to another realm, where audio storytelling reigns supreme and burrows itself deep into the hearts and ears of millions. I'm telling you, podcasting is where it's at. It's a labyrinth of genres and topics, offering creators an expansive playground to paint vivid narratives or dive into riveting discussions. But the real kicker is the sheer convenience of it all. Picture yourself commuting, working out, or just lounging around the house - boom, pop in those earbuds and soak up the audio goodness. It's like having a personal storyteller right there with you, weaving tales and provoking your thoughts. As a content creator, stepping into the realm of podcasting has allowed me to engage in deeper conversations, share my knowledge, and connect with my audience in a way that feels like I'm right there in the room with them. As the demand for audio content surges, podcasting offers us creators a golden opportunity to expand our reach and make our voices heard loud and clear.

But hey, hold onto your hats, because it's time to peek into the crystal ball and gaze upon the future of content consumption trends. Brace yourselves, folks, because technology is hurtling forward at warp speed, and it's dragging our preferences and behaviors along for the ride. We're talking artificial intelligence, virtual reality, and augmented reality, baby. These game-changers are reshaping the way we consume content and blurring the lines between the digital and physical worlds. And guess what? As content creators, we need to keep our finger on the pulse of these mind-blowing advancements if we want to stay hip and relevant. Imagine a world where viewers are transported into the shoes of the protagonist, interacting with characters in real-time, and even shaping the story themselves. This is the next level of content consumption, my friends, and it's got the power to revolutionize the very essence of content creation as we know it.

So, to wrap things up, this ever-evolving landscape of platforms and formats is an exhilarating playground for us content creators. Short-form videos, live streaming, podcasting - they all offer a smorgasbord of opportunities to captivate our audience, build an army of loyal fans, and make a lasting impact. By embracing these new platforms and formats, we're riding a wave of innovation, constantly evolving our craft, and shaping the future of content creation. As I stare into the unknown, I can't help but feel both excited and eager to uncover the uncharted secrets that will propel us to new, mind-bending heights in this dynamic world of content creation. Let's go conquer it together, my friends.

NICHE COMMUNITIES AND MICRO-INFLUENCERS

I can't even begin to express how amazed I am by the power and potential of niche communities and micro-influencers. Seriously, it's like a whole new world out there. Gone are the days of throwing out generic content and hoping it sticks with a wide audience. We are living in a time where niche communities and micro-influencers are completely changing the way content is created, consumed, and engaged with.

I think one of the main reasons niche communities are on the rise is because people crave connection with like-minded individuals. I mean, think about it. In this crazy fast-paced world, we're constantly bombarded with so much information that it can be overwhelming. We just want to find our tribe, a place where we feel like we belong and where our passions and experiences are understood. Niche communities offer a safe haven where individuals can connect with others who genuinely get them, whether it's a community dedicated to saving the environment, rocking vintage fashion, or rescuing cute little furry animals.

From a content creator's perspective, niche communities are like goldmines. Now, we don't have to aim for mass appeal and hope our content will speak to the right people. Nope, we can zoom in on a particular niche and tailor our content to meet the specific needs and desires of that community. By doing this, we not only increase the chances of our content being discovered, but we also create a stronger bond with our audience. It's all about that connection, baby!

And let's not forget about the micro-influencers. These guys are the secret sauce that brings these niche communities to life. Forget about those huge, distant celebrities with millions of followers. Micro-influencers have a smaller but oh-so-passionate audience. They know their niche inside out and can connect with their audience on a deep, personal level. They're like friends, or even peers, not some untouchable celebs. People trust them because they are seen as genuine and unbiased. And that, my friends, is pure gold.

For us content creators, collaborating with micro-influencers is like hitting the jackpot. By partnering with someone who has established themselves in a specific niche, we can tap into their audience and create content that really hits home. It not only increases the visibility of our content, but it also ups its credibility and trustworthiness. It's through these collaborations that we can expand our reach and build a super loyal following within these niche communities.

But hold on a second, folks. While all this excitement is going on, let's not forget that the game has changed. Traditional marketing strategies that relied on mass advertising and one-way communication are about as useful as a floppy disk. Audiences these days want interactive and personalized experiences. They want to be part of the conversation, not just bystanders.

So content creators, listen up. We have to adapt to this new landscape by embracing two-way communication and actively engaging with our audience. We're talking about hosting live Q&A sessions, jumping into online discussions, and responding to comments and messages. It's all about building that sense of community and getting invaluable feedback that shapes the future of our content.

And while we're at it, let's not forget the power of technology and data analytics. By analyzing audience demographics, interests, and behaviors, we can understand what makes our audience tick. Armed with this knowledge, we can create super targeted and relevant content that speaks directly to their desires. It's like we're mind-readers or something!

In conclusion, guys, niche communities and micro-influencers have completely changed the game for us content creators. We can't rely on generic content or old-school marketing strategies anymore. We have to embrace the power of niche communities, team up with awesome micro-influencers, and actively engage with our audience. It's all about creating content that hits deep and speaks to our people. So let's dive in and make our voices heard in this crazy, crowded digital space!

THE CONSTANT NEED FOR ADAPTATION

When I first embarked on my journey as a content creator, I was clueless about the wild ride that awaited me. I ignorantly believed that once I found my niche, my skills and content would stand the test of time. Oh, how wrong I was.

The world of content creation is like a chameleon, constantly changing its colors to survive and flourish. Platforms pop up and disappear faster than you can blink, algorithms take unexpected twists and turns, and audience tastes have more mood swings than a teenager. It's a wild and unpredictable world, my friends.

But here's the thing - embracing change is the key to success. Yeah, we humans tend to resist and dig our heels in when faced with something new. We're creatures of habit, always seeking comfort in familiarity. But if you want to rise above the crowd, you gotta learn to go with the flow. You gotta be willing to learn new things, try out new platforms, and experiment with fresh techniques.

As I dived deeper into the content creation universe, I realized that staying adaptable meant keeping one eye on emerging trends. It's all about observing, analyzing, and recalibrating your strategies. I became a detective, always seeking clues about the next big thing, trying to figure out what makes my audience tick. It's like being a content clairvoyant, predicting the shifts and adjusting my sails accordingly. It's a thrilling and suspenseful ride, let me tell you.

But staying ahead of the curve isn't just about having a prophetic crystal ball. It also means continuously upgrading your skills. The digital world moves at the speed of light, and as content creators, we gotta keep up. I'm not saying you gotta tear down your whole skill set and start from scratch. Nope. It's about expanding your arsenal, embracing new technologies and techniques that can take your content to the next level. Think of it as a creative superpower that you unleash upon the world.

Upskilling isn't just a chore - it's a rewarding adventure. It keeps you relevant, sure, but it also opens up new doors of creativity and innovation. With every new advancement in technology, we content creators get a whole new box of toys to play with. And when you're adaptable, you can harness these tools to push the boundaries of what's possible and leave your audience gasping for more.

Now, I ain't gonna lie to you - adapting to

the ever-changing landscape of content creation is no easy feat. It can be overwhelming and downright exhausting. But trust me, it's totally worth it. Embracing change and staying adaptable is the secret sauce that keeps my content fresh, my audience engaged, and my name on everyone's lips. It's through adaptability that I've opened doors to growth and collaboration, expanding my reach and creating content that resonates with more than just my mom.

To truly embrace adaptability, you gotta cultivate a growth mindset, my friend. Always be curious, thirsty for knowledge and new experiences. Stay open to feedback, even when it stings a little. And never forget the power of collaboration - there's so much to learn from others who see things from a different perspective.

So, my fellow content creators, buckle up. The only constant in this world is change, and we gotta ride that wave with confidence. By embracing adaptability, learning new skills, and staying one step ahead of the trends, we can leave an indelible mark on the ever-evolving world of content creation. Let's unleash our creative potential, captivate our audience, and make this world a little more colorful, one post at a time.

CHAPTER 12

Mental and Emotional Well-being

RECOGNIZING AND MANAGING BURNOUT

Man, I gotta tell ya, it hit me hard one day. I was sitting there, thinking about all the crap I've been through as a content creator, and it hit me like a ton of bricks. Burnout. I had fallen right into its trap without even realizing it. That's when I knew I had to do something about it. I couldn't just let it consume me.

So, I set out on a journey to figure out how the heck to deal with this burnout thing. I dug into research like a madman, talked to other creators who had been through it, and man, let me tell you, it was eye-opening.

First thing I learned was that you gotta recognize the signs of burnout. It's like this tornado that sucks you in and you don't even realize it until it's too late. You feel exhausted all the time, your motivation goes out the window, and don't even get me started on how damn irritable you become. Your productivity? Down the drain. It's like this never-ending cycle of trying to keep up with the expectations of your audience. It's a real recipe for disaster.

But here's the thing, self-care is the key, my friend. We've always been told to put our audience first, but that's a big ol' mistake. Taking care of yourself is crucial, not only for your sanity but for your creativity too. We gotta recognize our limits, take breaks when we need them, and do things that make us feel alive again. It may sound crazy, but stepping back from the grind is what's gonna save us from burning out.

And let's not forget about boundaries, man. We gotta draw the line. It's too damn easy to get sucked into this never-ending vortex of work. We gotta set some boundaries to protect ourselves, both in our personal lives and in our careers. Take some designated downtime, limit those work hours, and show some love to the people and things that matter to us. By doing that, we create this safe space to recharge and keep going in this crazy industry.

And you know what else? Stress is gonna be there, no matter what. It's just a fact of life as a content creator. But we can't let it consume us. We gotta manage that stress, dude. Meditate, exercise, lean on our fellow creators for support. Find those activities that bring us joy and help us stay present and calm. And if things get really rough, don't be afraid to seek help. Therapy, counseling, whatever it takes to keep our heads above water.

So, here's the deal, my friend. Burnout is a real monster in this industry. But we got the power to fight it. We gotta recognize the signs, take care of ourselves, set some boundaries, and manage that stress. It's not just about surviving as content creators, it's about enjoying the journey and finding fulfillment. I hope that by sharing my discoveries, other creators out there can avoid the burnout trap and find their own sense of happiness and success.

PRIORITIZING SELF-CARE

Mindfulness practices, my friend, they play a crucial role in keeping us grounded and present in our work. And let me tell you, incorporating meditation into my daily routine? Life-changing. I mean, seriously, just a few minutes every day to sit in stillness, focus on my breath, and silence those crazy racing thoughts? It's like hitting the reset button. I feel totally refreshed and ready to take on whatever challenges lie ahead. It's like a shot of espresso for the soul, ya know?

Now, there are a bunch of ways to practice mindfulness. You can use guided meditation apps, or you can simply find a quiet space to reflect. The point is, these practices can help us content creators find some balance and stay calm in the midst of all the chaos.

But self-care, my friend, it goes beyond just the mind. It's about taking care of our bodies, too. We spend so much time glued to our screens, it's important to find ways to get moving. Exercise, man, it not only boosts our energy levels, but it also enhances our creativity and focus. So, like, whether it's a morning yoga session or a quick dance break, we gotta find ways to incorporate movement into our daily routines. It's essential for our well-being and it helps prevent burnout. Trust me, I've learned that the hard way.

But self-care, bro, it's not just about taking care of ourselves - it's about nurturing those personal relationships outside of work, too. It's easy to get sucked into our projects and forget about the people who matter most. So, let's make time to connect, ya know? A phone call, a dinner date, even a heartfelt message - it can make a huge difference. Building and maintaining those solid personal relationships, man, they provide us with support and remind us that there's more to life than just work.

And hey, let's not forget about sleep, my friend. In this digital world that never sleeps, it's so tempting to sacrifice some shut-eye for more productivity. But research shows that getting enough sleep is crucial for our performance, creativity, and overall well-being. So, let's establish a bedtime routine, you know, incorporate some relaxation techniques and create a sleep-friendly environment. It's gonna do wonders for us.

I get it, man. As content creators, it feels impossible to make self-care a priority. But trust me on this one, neglecting our well-being only leads to burnout and a decline in the quality of our work. So, let's make a change. Let's prioritize mindfulness, exercise, sleep, and nurturing those personal relationships. Believe me, it's gonna bring balance, enhance our creativity, and help us thrive in this crazy content creator world.

In my own journey, bro, I've seen firsthand the power of self-care. By intentionally carving out time for myself, I've tapped into this wellspring of inspiration and produced content that's not only meaningful but sustainable. Taking care of myself, man, it's not just a luxury - it's a necessity. It allows me to pour my heart and soul into my work and into the lives of those who consume it. And yeah, it might take some adjustments and a shift in mind-set, but the rewards, my friend, they far outweigh the effort.

So, my fellow content creators, let's not forget to take care of ourselves in the midst of all this hustle and bustle. Our well-being is just as important as the content we create. By prioritizing mindfulness, exercise, sleep, and nurturing those personal rela-tionships, we can not only thrive in our roles but also live a fuller, more balanced life. Self-care, my friend, it's not a luxury - it's a necessity. It's what's gonna help us create, inspire, and flourish.

THE IMPACT OF SOCIAL MEDIA ON MENTAL HEALTH

Hey there, folks! Today, we're diving into the

complex and hush-hush topic of how social media can mess with our mental health. As creators, we're no strangers to the pull and power of these platforms, but we've gotta be real careful because they can really take a toll on our well-being. By talking about the potential downsides and figuring out ways to keep a healthy relationship with social media, we can hopefully avoid its harmful effects.

Let's kick it off with the allure of social media. In this crazy digital age, it's become a major part of our lives. From connecting with people, both personally and professionally, to networking in the online world, there are tons of opportunities. But for us content creators, it's a constant battle for attention and validation. The pressure to perform, the fear of missing out, and constantly comparing ourselves to others can really mess with our heads if we're not careful.

Now, let's talk about the dark side of social media. Yeah, it's got its perks, but it also comes with a lot of baggage. Research shows that excessive use can lead to feelings of depression, anxiety, and low self-esteem. The shiny, picture-perfect lives that people curate can make us feel like we're not measuring up or not worthy enough, and that's a major hit to our mental well-being. Plus, let's not forget about the online trolls and cyberbullying – those jerks can make everything even worse.

Okay, so how can we tell when social media is really messing with our heads? There are some tell-tale signs we should be on the lookout for. Feeling overwhelmed all the time, watching our self-esteem take a nosedive, getting caught up in comparing ourselves to others way too much, or struggling to separate our online and offline lives – all those are red flags. Once we recognize these signs, we can start taking action to protect our mental health.

One of the best things we can do is set some boundaries. Yep, we need to take charge and establish designated screen-free times, limit the amount of time we spend scrolling on social media, and create a safe space to disconnect from the online world. By sticking to these boundaries, we can regain control over our mental health while still reaping the benefits of social media as content creators.

Another essential part of staying sane on social media is curating our feeds. It's all about surrounding ourselves with positivity and inspiration rather than content that brings us down. Unfollow those accounts that make us feel like garbage and actively seek out content that uplifts and motivates us. By doing this, we can create an online environment that supports our mental well-being.

But wait, there's more! It's not just about the online connections. We also need to focus on cultivating meaningful relationships offline. Yeah, I know, as content creators, we spend tons of time connecting with people online, but it's important to balance it out. Spending quality time with loved ones, pursuing hobbies, or getting involved in community events can do wonders for our mental health. We're not just digital beings, after all – we need that face-to-face interaction to have a fulfilling life.

Now, here's a reminder we all need: self-care is non-negotiable. In this hustle-and-bustle content creation world, we often put ourselves last. But let's not forget that our mental health is priority number one. We've gotta make time for self-care practices like regular exercise, mindfulness, getting enough sleep, and doing things that make us happy. When we take care of ourselves, we're better equipped to handle the challenges of social media with strength and positivity.

And finally, let's not forget that we're not alone in this mental health battle. Reach out to friends, family, or even professionals who can lend a listening ear or offer some guidance. Connecting with others who understand the unique challenges we face as content creators can give us a fresh perspective and some much-needed support in maintaining a healthy relationship with social media.

To wrap things up, we can't ignore the potential harm social media can have on our mental health. But with the strategies we've covered – setting boundaries, curating our feeds, cultivating offline connections, prioritizing self-care, and seeking support – we can protect ourselves and thrive in the digital world. Stay strong, my fellow content creators, and let's keep that mental well-being in check while we rock it out online.

SEEKING SUPPORT AND PROFESSIONAL HELP

Let me tell you about a game-changer when it comes to seeking support and professional help as a content creator – therapy or counseling. Now, I know what you might be thinking – therapy, really? Isn't that for people with "real" problems? Well, hold on, because that couldn't be further from the truth. Therapy is like a secret weapon that gives us a safe space to dive deep into our thoughts and emotions, helping us uncover any hidden roadblocks that might be messing with our creative groove.

Picture this – you're on the content creation grind, juggling deadlines, battling self-doubt, and dealing with the never-ending pressure to come up with fresh ideas. It's enough to drive anyone bonkers, right? But that's where therapy swoops in to save the day. Through therapy, we get to learn badass coping techniques that we can add to our stress-fighting arsenal. We're talking about mindfulness exercises, deep breathing wizardry, and even some fancy stuff like cognitive-behavioral therapy (CBT). With these tools in our back pocket, we become unstoppable forces of resilience, taking on any creative challenge that dares to stand in our way.

But therapy isn't only about stress management and keeping our sanity intact. It also gives us the chance to open up about our deepest fears, insecurities, and that pesky little voice inside our heads that shouts "imposter!" whenever we dare to show our true creative selves. As content creators, we're constantly exposing our work to the world, inviting criticism and judgment. It's easy to get sucked into a black hole of self-doubt. That's where therapy steps in to help us slay our inner demons and build a healthy dose of self-worth. Ta-da! Say goodbye to negative self-perception and hello to a confident, self-assured mindset.

Now, let's talk about the mother of all creative buzzkills – imposter syndrome. It's that nagging feeling that we're all just frauds, faking our way through success and lucking into our achievements. Pretty soul-crushing, right? Well, guess what? Therapy can tackle imposter syndrome head-on, armed with tricks and strategies to flip those negative thoughts on their heads. By reevaluating our accomplishments and embracing our capabilities, we start seeing ourselves as the badass content creators we truly are.

But hey, therapy isn't the only path to success and sanity. Seeking professional guidance is another game-changing move. Think about it – the content creation industry is a wild ride, like a rollercoaster that never stops. Keeping up with trends, algorithm changes, and managing contracts can give even the savviest creator a massive headache. That's when professionals with expertise in our field become our heroes. They guide us through the intricacies of the industry, providing insights that can skyrocket our chances of success. Trust me, having a pro by your side is like having a cheat code to navigate the wildest parts of the content creation world.

And there's more! Professionals can help us tackle other challenges too. You know, the real-life stuff that kinda gets in the way of our creative zen. Like managing our bewildering finances when income streams are as steady as a rollercoaster ride. Financial advisors who understand the content creation whirlpool can save the day with budgeting and planning strategies that make sense. And let's not forget about public relations whizzes who can teach us the art of managing our online image, handling brand collaborations, and handling any PR disasters that may come our way.

Now, hold onto your creative hats, because I'm about to drop a nugget of genius. Every content creator needs a mentor – a wise, experienced soul who walks beside us, guiding our way through this chaotic journey. A mentor is like a beacon of light, sharing their hard-earned knowledge, giving us that extra boost of confidence, and challenging us to reach new heights. Having a mentor is like having a personal guru who knows the ropes and can help us dodge all the potholes along the way. With their guidance, we can stay on course and achieve our wildest dreams.

So, my fellow content creators, here's the bottom line – seeking support and professional help is the secret sauce for success in our crazy world. Therapy and counseling give us a safe space to unpack our thoughts and equip us with killer coping strategies. Professionals who specialize in our field unlock secret doors to success, providing insights that level up our game. And mentors? They're the superheroes who accompany us on this wild ride, providing guidance and cheering us on. Embrace support, my friends, and watch yourself soar to new creative heights!

BALANCING WORK AND PERSONAL LIFE

You know what it's like, right? As content creators, we get sucked into this crazy, demanding world of work, always juggling deadlines, trying to engage with our audience, and pumping out top-notch content. It's like we're in a never-ending race for success, constantly pushing ourselves to the limit. But you know what suffers when we get caught up in the whirlwind? Our personal lives. We end up feeling burnt out, disconnected from the things that truly matter. It's a real bummer.

But fear not, my fellow content creators! I've got your back. In this chapter, I'm diving deep into the crucial topic of maintaining a healthy work-life balance. I'm gonna spill all the beans and give you some killer strategies and insights that will empower you to prioritize your personal well-being alongside your professional commitments. You ready? Let's do this!

PART 1: THE ART OF TIME MANAGEMENT

Time, my friend, is a precious resource. We all have it, but more often than not, it slips right through our fingers without us even noticing. To achieve that sweet spot of work and personal life balance, you gotta become a master of time management. Trust me, it's a game-changer.

One super helpful technique I've discovered is

making a daily schedule. By carving out specific time slots for work, relaxation, and personal activities, I can make sure I'm giving enough attention to each aspect of my life. It keeps me organized and stops me from either overworking or neglecting my personal commitments. Talk about killing two birds with one stone!

And hey, don't forget about all the cool productivity tools and apps out there. They're a game-changer too! Seriously, they can turbocharge your time management skills. I'm talking about handy dandy reminders, alarms, and even task trackers. There are so many to choose from, like Todoist, Trello, or good ol' Google Calendar. Test 'em out and find the one that vibes with you.

Part 2: Establishing Boundaries

Now, this is where things can get a bit tricky for us content creators. Setting boundaries between work and personal life can sometimes feel like trying to herd a bunch of cats. It's tough, especially with smartphones and all the access we have to our work. But fear not, my friend. I've got some tricks up my sleeve.

First things first, setting clear boundaries is a must. You gotta communicate with your clients or collaborators about your availability and establish some "off" hours. This helps create a mutual understanding of when you're available to work and when you need some downtime. It's a win-win situation, trust me. No more burnout and more time for yourself and your loved ones.

But hold up, we gotta set boundaries within ourselves too. Yep, you heard me right. Resist the temptation to always be glued to your phone, constantly checking work emails during your personal time. Make yourself a cozy little physical space, like a separate office or a cool workspace, where you can buckle down and focus. And when you step away from it, detach yourself, my friend. Detach.

Part 3: Prioritizing Personal Well-being

Let's talk about something that's often forgotten

in the whirlwind of content creation – you! Taking care of yourself is a priority, not a luxury. Repeat after me: self-care is not selfish. Got it? Good.

So, to maintain that sweet work-life balance, you better start prioritizing some serious self-care. Get some exercise, meditate, do whatever floats your boat for relaxation. Carve out a little time each day to recharge and rejuvenate. Trust me, you'll thank yourself later.

Oh, and don't forget about building up your support system. It's essential for navigating the ups and downs of this balancing act. Surround yourself with folks who get it, who understand the demands of your profession. Get into some networking groups or online communities where you can share experiences and strategies with other content creators in the same boat. There's power in numbers, my friend.

Conclusion

Finding that perfect work-life balance isn't some mythical creature only spoken of in old legends.

It's absolutely within your reach. But it takes some effort, dedication, and a little trial and error. Follow the strategies I've shared here, adapt as needed, and you'll be well on your way to cultivating a fulfilling and balanced life as a content creator. You got this!

CHAPTER 13

The Journey of Content Creation

EMBRACING THE CREATIVE PROCESS

You know what's wild? The creative process. It's like this crazy adventure that takes you on a roller-coaster of emotions, from excitement to doubt and everything in between. But let me tell you, it's worth every single twist and turn.

When I first started on this creative journey, I had no clue what I was getting myself into. It was like stepping into the great unknown, a mix of nerves and anticipation. I mean, who was I to think I could create something that others would actually connect with? But boy, I couldn't have been more wrong. This creative journey turned out to be one of the most mind-blowing and life-changing experiences ever.

It all starts with an idea, a tiny little seed planted in the garden of our minds. At first, it seems fragile and insignificant, but with some nurturing and TLC, that seed has the potential to grow into something extraordinary. It's like watching a flower bloom before your eyes. Awe-inspiring, really. That initial stage is a mix of curiosity and wonder as we dive headfirst into exploring all the possibilities our idea holds.

But let me tell you, it's not all rainbows and sunshine. Oh no, there are challenges lurking around every corner. Doubt starts to creep in, and suddenly you're questioning if your ideas are even worth pursuing. Will anyone care? Will your creation get lost in the vast sea of content out there? It's a tough pill to swallow, my friend. But in those dark moments, you gotta trust in yourself and your instincts. Take a leap of faith and believe that your ideas matter.

And that's when the real magic happens. Bringing our ideas to life is an absolute thrill. It's like wielding a superpower, transforming our thoughts into something tangible that can be shared with the world. Whether it's writing, creating videos, or designing websites, the act of creation is incredibly fulfilling. There's a deep sense of satisfaction that comes from seeing your ideas take shape and knowing that you've made a meaningful contribution.

But listen, it's not all smooth sailing. Nope, not even close. Along the way, you'll stumble and fall, doubting every step you take. It's in those moments that you truly learn what you're made of. Do you give up, swallowed by fear? Or do you pick yourself up and keep pushing forward? The answer lies in your ability to embrace the challenges and setbacks as opportunities to grow and learn. It ain't easy, but it's necessary.

And here's something wild: the creative process has this crazy ability to push us out of our comfort zones. It forces us to confront our fears and limitations head-on. And yeah, it can get uncomfortable real quick. But let me tell you something, it's in those vulnerable moments that we truly blossom. Through our creative pursuits, we tap into our true potential and discover parts of ourselves we never even knew existed.

Through my own creative journey, I've come to realize that it's not just about the end result. It's about the whole adventure, the ups, the downs, and all the growth in between. It's about testing your limits, pushing yourself beyond what you thought possible. It's about embracing the unknown, navigating through uncertainty with your head held high. It's about finding joy and fulfillment in the act of creating, regardless of the outcome.

So let me tell you, my friend, embrace the wild ride that is the creative process. Embrace the ups, the downs, and everything in between. Allow yourself to be vulnerable, take risks, and trust your instincts. And most importantly, inspire others to embark on their own creative journey. Because in the end, it's through our creations that we leave a lasting impact on the world.

LESSONS LEARNED FROM SETBACKS

When I started my journey as a content creator, I was plagued with self-doubt and a gnawing fear of failure. It was like a dark cloud hanging over me, sucking the joy out of my every creation. I spent countless hours pouring my heart and soul into crafting what I thought was the perfect content, only to be greeted with minimal engagement or worse, critical comments that felt like punches to my confidence.

Those setbacks, however, taught me some real-deal invaluable lessons. Looking back, I realize that they were more than just roadblocks – they were opportunities for growth and self-discovery.

The first lesson that hit me like a bolt of lightning was the importance of authenticity. In this day and age, it's easy to get swept up in trends and mimic what's already popular. But lemme tell ya, setbacks forced me to take a hard look at my content and ask myself, "Am I being true to who I really am?" It was a wake-up call to shed the imitations and embrace my unique voice. And lemme tell ya, that's when the magic happened. When I started creating content that I was truly passionate about, rather than trying to fit into someone else's mold, I found myself standing out like a flamingo in a flock of pigeons. It was liberating to let my freak flag fly, to experiment with new ideas and formats that genuinely excited me.

Another big lesson was resilience – the superhero power we all wish we had. See, setbacks can knock the wind outta your sails and make you feel like giving up. But lemme tell ya, it's in those moments of adversity that the tough get going. Instead of letting setbacks define me, I used 'em as fuel to ignite my determination. Each setback became an opportunity for growth and improvement. Yeah, they made me stumble, but they sure as hell made me stronger. Like a phoenix rising from the ashes, I learned to brush off the dirt, stand up tall, and keep pushing forward.

And can I tell you about the power of seeking support and feedback? As content creators, we can easily get stuck in our own little bubble, thinking we're the hottest thing since sliced bread. But setbacks have a way of smacking us back to reality, reminding us that we ain't got it all figured out. I learned to reach out to my fellow creators, mentors, and even my audience, asking for their thoughts and constructive criticism. It was like opening the curtains to a whole new world. Their fresh perspectives and insights helped me see my content in a different light, and boy did it make a difference. Plus, it created this awesome sense of community and collaboration that made me feel like I was part of something bigger.

But you know what? The most important lesson of all was the one that hit me right in the feels – self-care and mental well-being. Lemme tell ya, the pressure to constantly churn out mind-blowing content and meet unrealistic expectations can do a number on your mental health. Those setbacks made me realize that I had been neglecting myself, putting my well-being on the back burner. And lemme tell ya, it was a wake-up call of epic proportions. I started paying attention to my mind and body, taking breaks when I needed 'em, stepping away from the screen, and doing things that rejuvenated my creativity. Turns out, when I started prioritizing self-care, my content reflected that too. It became infused with this authenticity and passion that I didn't even know I had.

So, dear fellow content creators, listen up. I know setbacks can feel like a punch in the gut, like a roadblock you can't avoid. But lemme tell ya, they ain't the end of the road. They're just bumps on the journey to success. Embrace 'em, learn from 'em, and use 'em as stepping stones to becoming the badass creator you were meant to be. Seek support, take care of yourself, and above all, believe in your unique voice and the power of your content. Trust me, the road may be bumpy, but damn, those lessons you learn along the way make it all worthwhile.

FINDING PURPOSE AND MEANING

You know, when it comes to content creation, it's not just about catchy headlines and a massive following. It's so much more than that. It's about digging deep into our souls, finding our passions, and sharing them in a way that really connects with others. It's about unraveling our stories and putting them out there for the world to see. And let me tell you, when you tap into that, it's like finding the missing piece of the puzzle. Suddenly, you start to question the impact of your work, and whether it really matters in the grand scheme of things.

I remember when I first started out on this journey, all I really wanted to do was entertain people. I wanted to make them laugh and give them a break from their everyday lives. But over time, I realized there was more to it. I started questioning the purpose of my work. Was I really making a difference? That's when I stumbled upon some research studies that completely shook me to my core.

One study in particular caught my attention.

The researchers at Stanford found that creating content that helps others, what they call "prosocial" content, not only gives the content creator a sense of purpose, but it also has a positive impact on the audience. It turns out, when people consume this prosocial content, they experience a surge of positivity and are more likely to do good things themselves. It's like a ripple effect of kindness and compassion.

That study really struck a chord with me. It made me realize that content creation has the power to spread positivity and inspire change. It challenged me to shift my focus from just entertaining to creating content that really makes a lasting impact. I wanted to start conversations, raise awareness, and motivate people to take action.

But let me tell you, finding that purpose and meaning in content creation is not an easy task. It requires some serious reflection. We have to understand ourselves and what we're passionate about. And we also have to understand the needs and desires of our audience. It's about digging deep and embracing our uniqueness, because that's what really resonates with people.

And you know what? The research studies weren't the only thing that inspired me along this journey. I learned so much from fellow content creators who had found their purpose and meaning in what they do. Take Sarah, for example. She started a YouTube channel all about mental health. She shared her own struggles with anxiety and depression and created a space where others could find support. And let me tell you, her vulnerability touched the lives of so many people.

Listening to Sarah's story really opened my eyes to the power of authenticity in content creation. Sharing our true selves, our struggles, and our vulnerabilities creates a safe space for others to do the same. In a world that's obsessed with perfection, people are craving real connections and stories that remind them they're not alone.

As content creators, we have the privilege and responsibility to inspire and uplift others through our work. We can use our platforms to shed light on important issues, challenge the status quo, and empower people to chase their dreams. We can create content that sparks conversations, promotes empathy, and brings people from all walks of life together.

But let me tell you, finding fulfillment in all of this isn't just going to happen overnight. We have to approach content creation with intentionality and a genuine desire to make a difference. We have to ask ourselves what impact we want to have on the world and how our unique perspectives and stories can contribute to that.

So, my fellow content creators, let's embark on this journey together. Let's uncover our passions and tell our stories in a way that leaves a lasting impact. Let's embrace the power of authenticity and connect with our audience on a profound level. And most importantly, let's remember that our creative work has the power to change lives and make the world a better place.

Because at the end of the day, it's in this exploration and pursuit of purpose that we find true fulfillment and meaning as content creators. It's knowing that what we do has the power to shape lives and make a real impact. So let's go out there and do it. Let's change the world, one piece of content at a time.

CELEBRATING SUCCESS AND MILESTONES

Let me tell you about my journey as a content creator, my friend. It's a wild ride, full of twists and turns, doubts and triumphs. But through it all, I've come to appreciate the importance of reflection and celebration. It's like taking a step back and soaking it all in – the highs, the lows, and everything in between. And let me tell you, it's the best way to find motivation and a true sense of fulfillment in what I do.

Celebrating success and milestones is a game-changer, my friend. It's not just about popping the champagne and patting yourself on the back (although that's always fun). It's about seeing how far you've come, recognizing the growth you've achieved. As content creators, we're always evolving, experimenting, and pushing ourselves to the limit. Each project is a chance to learn something new, to refine our skills and bring our visions to life. So, by reflecting on our victories, big and small, we get a glimpse of our own progress. And let me tell you, that boosts our confidence like nothing else. It's a reminder that we're on the right track, headed straight for that dream destination.

But let me share a little secret with you, my friend. Back when I was just starting out, I didn't pay much attention to those small wins. I was too focused on the end goal, the big prize. It was like I had tunnel vision, ignoring all the little stepping stones along the way. But let me tell you, that kind of mindset can really mess you up. It wasn't until I realized the damage it was causing that I shook myself out of it. I started recognizing even the tiniest accomplishments – hitting a certain number of subscribers, getting positive feedback from viewers, nailing a new editing trick. You know what happened? It was like throwing gasoline on a fire, my friend. Each win fueled my determination, my hunger for more success. Suddenly, I wasn't just waiting to reach the finish line – I was enjoying the whole damn journey.

And here's the thing, my friend. Celebrating success isn't just about us as individuals. It's about building a community, a family of content creators who lift each other up. We're all in this together, after all. By sharing our achievements, whether it's on social media, through collaborations, or at networking events, we inspire others and create chances for mutual celebration. It's a beautiful cycle, my friend. Celebrating each other's wins fuels our collective growth, our shared inspiration. It's like a big love fest for content creators, where we're all cheering each other on, helping each other reach new heights.

But let me be real with you, my friend. There were times in my journey where I doubted myself. Moments when I wondered if all my hard work was just disappearing into the void. It was during those dark times that celebrating success became my lifeline. Looking back at the milestones I'd reached, the positive feedback I'd received, and the growth I'd experienced – that was my wake-up call.

It reminded me that what I was doing mattered, that I was making a difference with my work. And you know what? It gave me the strength to push through those challenges, to keep creating content that truly touched people's hearts.

Reflecting on our personal achievements is an ongoing process, my friend. It's like taking a breather in the middle of this non-stop roller-coaster and appreciating just how far we've come. We have to revisit our past projects, analyze the impact we've made, and give ourselves a well-deserved pat on the back. That's how we gain a deeper understanding of our own journey, how we keep that fire burning inside us. And let me tell you, it's no small thing, my friend. Celebrating success, no matter how big or small, is what propels us forward. It's what drives us to achieve even greater things.

Now, I get it. In the grand scheme of things, celebrating success might not seem like a big deal. It pales in comparison to the great mountains we want to conquer. But my friend, let me tell you this – those small victories? They're what leads us straight to the top. Embracing the journey, acknowledging our progress, celebrating every step of the way – that's what sets us up for the big wins. So, as content creators, let's never underestimate the power of celebration. Let's embrace it, my friend. Let's unlock our full potential and bask in the joy of our creative endeavors.

WORDS OF INSPIRATION AND ENCOURAGEMENT

Listen up, folks. I've got something important to tell you. You are capable of greatness. Seriously, each and every one of us has something special inside of us that can be transformed into something incredible. So, never underestimate the power that lies within you to create content that captivates and inspires others. Let your individuality shine through your work, my friends.

Now, I know that even the most passionate content creators sometimes doubt themselves. It's rough when you feel like the road ahead is filled with uncertainty and obstacles. But let me tell you, it's during these moments that you need to believe in yourself the most. Believe in your abilities, your dreams, and the impact you can make. Always remember why you started on this journey in the first place, and let that be your guiding light, pushing you forward through anything that stands in your way.

And let me tell you, there will be obstacles. Rejection, criticism, creative blocks - they're all part of the game. But don't let them discourage you. Instead, view them as opportunities for growth and learning. Embrace them and use them to fuel your determination. Trust me, my friends, those hurdles are just stepping stones towards your ultimate vision.

Now, here's some practical advice I've got for you: never stop learning. The content creation world is always changing, always evolving. So, you've got to stay curious and open-minded. Keep seeking out new knowledge and skills. Go to workshops, take online courses, dive into books that challenge the way you think. And please, surround yourself with like-minded individuals who inspire you to be better. Trust me, it makes all the difference.

Oh, and don't forget about self-care. I know this gig can be demanding, sometimes blurring the lines between work and personal life. But you've got to find that balance and take care of yourself. Take breaks when you need them. Recharge your creativity by exploring new hobbies or just getting out in nature. And, for goodness sake, nurture your relationships with your loved ones. A healthy mind and body are essential for producing your best work.

Now, let's talk about something that can get a little tricky in this digital age. It's easy to get caught up in the numbers game, you know? How many likes, followers, and views you've got can start to consume you. But here's the thing - external validation shouldn't be the be-all and end-all of your success. Instead, focus on the impact you're making, the lives you're touching, and the connections you're forming with your audience. That, my friends, is what truly matters.

And lastly, don't be afraid to take risks and step outside of your comfort zone. Sometimes, the greatest breakthroughs and masterpieces come from moments of uncertainty and exploration. Embrace experimentation and allow yourself to make mistakes. Failure doesn't define you, it just shows that you're on the path to growth and discovery.

So, as I wrap up this little chat, I want you to remember this: you have the power to create content that moves people, inspires change, and shapes the world. Embrace your unique voice, believe in yourself, and keep pushing through challenges. The world needs your stories, insights, and creativity. So go out there, my fellow aspiring content creators, and make your mark on this ever-evolving landscape. It won't always be easy, but with passion, dedication, and an unwavering belief in yourself, you will unlock untold secrets and create pure magic through your content.

www.ingramcontent.com/pod-product-compliance
Lightning Source LLC
Chambersburg PA
CBHW020318160726
47992CB00004B/1589